The Defiant Muse

HISPANIC FEMINIST POEMS
FROM THE MIDDLE AGES
TO THE PRESENT

THE DEFIANT MUSE
Series Editor, Angel Flores

The Defiant Muse: Hispanic Feminist Poems from the Middle Ages to the Present
Edited and with an introduction by Ángel Flores and Kate Flores

The Defiant Muse: French Feminist Poems from the Middle Ages to the Present
Edited and with an introduction by Domna C. Stanton

The Defiant Muse: German Feminist Poems from the Middle Ages to the Present
Edited and with an introduction by Susan L. Cocalis

The Defiant Muse: Italian Feminist Poems from the Middle Ages to the Present
Edited by Beverly Allen, Muriel Kittel, and Keala Jane Jewell and with an introduction by Beverly Allen

The Defiant Muse

HISPANIC FEMINIST POEMS FROM THE MIDDLE AGES TO THE PRESENT

A BILINGUAL ANTHOLOGY

EDITED AND WITH AN INTRODUCTION BY
ANGEL FLORES AND KATE FLORES

THE FEMINIST PRESS
AT THE CITY UNIVERSITY OF NEW YORK
NEW YORK

89 88 87 86   6 5 4 3 2 1

Permission acknowledgments begin on page 146.

Cover and text design by Gilda Hannah
Typeset by Weinglas Typography Inc.
Manufactured by Banta Co.

This publication is made possible, in part, by public
funds from the New York State Council on the Arts.

Library of Congress Cataloging-in-Publication Data
Main entry under title:
Hispanic feminist poems from the Middle Ages to the
    present.
    (The defiant muse)
    English and Spanish.
    1. Feminist poetry, Spanish—Translations into
English.   2. Feminist poetry, Spanish American—
Translation into English.   3. English Poetry—
Translations from Spanish.   4. Feminist poetry,
Spanish.   5. Feminist poetry, Spanish American.
I. Flores, Angel, 1900–   . II. Flores, Kate.
III. Series.
PQ6267.E5F454   1985   861'.008'09287   85-16294
ISBN 0-935312-47-1
ISBN 0-935312-54-4 (pbk.)

Another way to be human and free.
Another way to be.

Rosario Castellanos

CONTENTS

PUBLISHER'S PREFACE

The Feminist Press is proud to publish this set of anthologies of feminist poetry, the first bilingual collection of its kind. When Domna C. Stanton proposed the project to The Press in 1983, I immediately responded that it was "a natural" for The Press, and a critical publication in women's studies that was long overdue. To be sure, the idea for the series and the actual work began years earlier. In 1976, Kate Flores urged Ángel, her husband, to collaborate on an anthology, not simply of women's poetry, which had been sporadically included in the more than twenty volumes of verse he had edited, but specifically of feminist poetry, which had never been done. However, as the enormity of the undertaking became apparent, they enlarged the original scope from one to four volumes, each to be devoted to a major language, and contacted Domna C. Stanton for French, Susan Cocalis for German, and Beverly Allen and Muriel Kittel for Italian. In common, these editors agreed upon the general conception of the volumes; independently, over a period of several years, they did extensive research in libraries at home and in the countries of origin. That arduous process led to a "re-vision" of poets whose feminism had been ignored or suppressed. Far more important, it led to the discovery of numerous poets whose work remains unknown in their own country to this day. Thanks to these editors, the poetry can now have the audience it deserves.

Reading each volume produces the exciting awareness of a strong national tradition of feminist poetry, dating back to "the dark ages." Together, the anthologies confirm the existence of many common themes and threads that connect women beyond differences of class and culture, time and place. For that inspiring vision, the editors of this series, like those of us at The Feminist Press, can be proud...and joyful.

INTRODUCTION

The word feminist has different meanings, depending on whose ears it falls upon. To some it connotes a woman who marches in parades carrying placards, burns bras, chains herself to fenceposts. Others think of a person—female or male—more acutely aware than most of inequities in the social order that work to the disadvantage of women, and, inevitably, of men as well; just as mistreatment of blacks, for example, works inevitably to the detriment of all members of their society. As Barbara McClintock, 1983 Nobel laureate in chemistry, remarked: ''I am not a feminist, but I am always gratified when barriers are broken down—against women, blacks, Jews. It helps us all.'' One need not be a feminist to be sensitive to the concerns of women.

But sensitivity, perhaps, is not enough. A feminist is willing to address those concerns, and to speak out about them. This requires courage, even at this very late date when everyone, everywhere, presumably, recognizes the existence of the subordination of women and the need to eliminate it. Even today there are university women who keep their feminism to themselves, perhaps out of fear of academic reprisal, or a sense that the system is too entrenched to be changed.

To be a feminist means to be not only sensitive to the reality of women's lives, but courageous enough to do something about it, to speak out, to criticize.

One of the provinces of poetry is just such criticism; poetry is a sensitive, courageous criticism of life. On this view, feminist poetry is a criticism of women's lives, and of the injustices women have suffered, in various times and places, as a consequence of their sex. It is poetry not necessarily by marchers and activists. On the contrary, few feminist poets have been directly involved in feminist movements, which are fairly recent, whereas feminist poetry is very old.

In compiling this anthology we have looked for records of inequity—testimony, as it were, of instances of women's oppression to be found in the annals of Hispanic poetry.

Such oppression has existed at all times and in all societies, but over the centuries women's issues have changed even as societies have changed.

In medieval times, for example, men were constantly at war. Taking up arms was considered noble, and war the highest good, the vindication of men's honor. It distinguished them from women, who were excluded from military pursuits and thus inescapably inferior. A man with daughters and no sons to send to battle felt disgraced. A popular ballad of this period, ''The Girl Warrior,'' tells of a man with seven daughters, one of whom redeems his honor by donning battle gear and proving her valor on the battlefield. The poem is feminist in bespeaking the unfairness of women's exclusion from the "honor" of military service when women were demonstrably as "honorable" as men.

Before the invention of the printing press in the fifteenth century, such anonymous ballads and songs were the principal form of communication in Europe, carried by minstrels from town to town. Repeated and embroidered upon, they were particularly popular throughout the Hispanic peninsula from the thirteenth to the sixteenth centuries; indeed some are still sung not only in Spain but in Spanish America, as well as the Near East and Africa, where Sephardic Jews carried the medieval Spanish language when they where expelled from Spain.

Most of the songs and ballads dealt with the exploits, in war and in love, of the national heroes—King Arthur and his Knights of the Round Table, Charlemagne and his Peers, the Spanish hero El Cid and his warriors. But some told of women abandoned for the battlefield, or hinted at other oppressive customs, at a time when women had few choices in life except to take the vows of either marriage or the church—neither, apparently, particularly attractive. Frequently, one or the other was forced upon them, sometimes as children, by tyrannical fathers who were also often guilty of incest.

We begin this anthology with some of these old songs (*canciones*) and ballads (*romances*), which may be considered among the earliest feminist poems in Spanish, culled from the songbooks, or *Cancioneros* and *Romanceros*, which began to be compiled in the fifteenth century. On the whole, these were all-male preserves, almost devoid of women's names, though an early *Cancionero* by Martínez de Burgos compiled in the 1460s included a religious poem by one María Sarmiento that may have been written as early as 1428 (only the first two lines and last stanza have survived). Among the thousand songs in Hernando del Castillo's *Cancionero general* (1511) we find a brief Latin poem ascribed to Una Dama, an anonymous "Question to Diego Nuñez by a Lady," and two *motes* or poetic mottoes, one by Catalina Manrique and one by Marina Manuel. Only the name of **Florencia Pinar*** (late fifteenth century) stands out. With three poems described as "Songs," she marks the transition from oral culture to literacy or written culture, and the emergence of women as poets.

Literacy, however, was long denied to women. During the Middle Ages almost all learning was confined to men, and the Church, the dominant social force, considered women incapable of literacy, mentally as well as morally inferior to men. Indeed, the entire medieval age was characterized by a strong misogyny, with numerous treatises warning against women and the sin of lust, such as *Disciplina clericalis* (c. 1100). These were especially prominent in Spain; examples include the *Book of the Deceits and*

---

*The names of poets whose works are included in this volume appear in boldface type at first mention.

Lechery of Women (1253), *El Corbacho* (c. 1466) by the Archpriest of Talavera, and Luis de Lucena's *Repetición de amores* (c.1497).

As one of the most recalcitrantly masculinist countries, with one of the richest poetic traditions, Spain provides a vivid theater for the study of feminist poetry against the background of its long and dramatic history.

In fact, on the Iberian peninsula songs and poems by women date from the time it was a colony of the Roman Empire, and Latin its official language. The names of some of these women have come down to us: Pola Argentaria, lauded by her contemporary Martial (40 B.C.–104 A.D.) and centuries later by Lope de Vega; the poet and Stoic philosopher Teofila; and Serena, an avid reader of Homer and Virgil.

The fall of the Roman Empire and ensuing invasions brought a commingling of cultures, mainly Christian, Arabic, and Hebraic, leading eventually to the transformation of Vulgar Latin into three new languages—Spanish, Catalan, and Galician—which gradually infused Arabic and Hebraic poetry. Thus two or four lines in Hebrew or Spanish—little poetic units called *jarchas*—were often added to Arabic strophic poems known as *moaxajas*. *Jarchas*, the earliest lyrical expression in the Spanish language, date from about the eleventh century. They were charming little love songs for a girl to sing, ingenuously reprimanding her admirer's boldness or lamenting his absence, expressing sadness at his departure or, less often, joy in his presence. Sometimes they invoked nature, as in dawn songs voicing dread of the coming of dawn after a night together. These *alboradas* suggest how ancient is woman's need for constancy and fidelity:

> Lovely dawn
> tell me where you come from.
> Already I know that you love someone else,
> you love me not.

Jarchas belong to the most characteristic genre of the early European lyric in the vernacular: women's folk songs, which also include the German *Frauenlied*, the French *chanson de femmes*, the Castilian and Catalan *cantar de doncella*, and the Galician-Portuguese *cantiga d'amigo* (friend song) of the thirteenth and fourteenth centuries. Indeed, some scholars believe the lyric had its beginnings in the songs of women many centuries earlier, and that at least some of the lyrics to be found in the *Cancioneros* were originally composed by women and attributed to the men who collected, refined, or glossed them. Women's folk songs were also sung by wandering minstrels (*juglares*) skilled at adapting them to the needs of their trade, which included few women.

The Galician-Portuguese *cantigas d'amigo* were distinguished from men's love songs, *cantigas de amor*, usually addressed to a lofty and unattainable lady in the manner of the Provençal troubadours, and from the religious *cantigas de Santa María*. Always plaintive and sad, the *cantigas d'amigo* are the loveliest and most memorable of the three types of songs, suffused as they are with the delicate sensibilities of women abandoned, betrayed, and lonely. One, attributed to Nuno Fernández de Turneol (fl. 1225), conveys the emotions of a girl who goes to receive twenty ships returning soldiers from war only to find her lover not among them.

While a few of the *cantigas d'amigo* were marked Anon., none were ascribed to women at a time when only upper-class women were literate, and the common people mostly unlettered. Indeed, literacy was one of the jewels of the nobility, who enjoyed flaunting it. On the Iberian peninsula every kingdom had its court poets, strongly influenced by the Provençal troubadours and the Galician-Portuguese *cantigas*. The court poets included numbers of women, among whom the composition of music and poetry became very fashionable. Bertranda de Forcadels organized a veritable Parnassus at the court of King Martin of Aragon. Guillerma de Sales, wife of the troubadour Count Hugo, established a lively literary center in their Mataplana castle. Queen Ana, wife of Enrique II, and Vayona, so called probably because born in Bayonne, France, were among the many court poets who flourished with the reign of the poet-king Juan II (1406–1458) of Castile. Florencia Pinar was doubtless close to if not actually a part of the court of Ferdinand and Isabella, whose reign began in 1479. Though little is known of her life, she must certainly have been educated, and possibly aware of the Italian currents (especially Petrarch) that had entered Spain during the fifteenth century.

Among other learned women attached to the court, Pinar was no exception. Beatriz Galindo (1475–1514), a philosopher and accomplished linguist, taught Latin to Queen Isabella. Called La Latina, she formed a circle at the palace where she read and discussed her *Comentarios sobre Aristóteles* and other classical writers. She also founded a hospital in Madrid called Hospital La Latina.

Another erudite woman was Luisa Sigea (1530–1560), known as La Toledana (Woman from Toledo), who at sixteen wrote a letter to Pope Paul III in Latin, Greek, Arabic, and Syrian, and whose long poem in Latin, *Cintra*, published in Paris, won her recognition throughout Europe. The king of Portugal, Dom Manuel, invited her to Lisbon where she presided over a literary circle and tutored the Infanta Domna María.

The Golden Age of Spain (mid-sixteenth to mid-seventeenth centuries) saw a certain reaction against the generally antifemale attitude characteristic of the Middle Ages. Both Cervantes (1547–1616) and Lope de Vega (1562–1635) often depicted women not as weak, wicked, and lecherous, but as strong, heroic, and virtuous; and both admired their contemporary St. Teresa of Ávila (1515–1582), the many-sided genius whose autobiography has been compared to St. Augustine's *Confessions*, and who wrote mystical poems as well as such major prose works as *Road to Perfection* (1565) and *The Interior Castle* (1577). An uncompromising reformer of what she considered lax standards, she sought a return to rigorous discipline and self-denial. Traveling throughout Spain despite bad weather, bad roads, filthy inns, and harassment of the Church bureaucracy (permissions granted and revoked, lawsuits, imprisonment), she established more than twenty convents of Barefoot Carmelite nuns and, in collaboration with St. John of the Cross, fifteen monasteries of friars. Striving to have her barefoot nuns treated no worse than the shod friars, she counseled them and herself that "patient endurance/attaineth all things."

The tempestuous Catalina de Erauso (1592–1625), known as La Monja Alférez (the Nun Ensign), competed with the conquistadores in exploring the New World. Her autobiography describing twenty years of adventures dressed as a man makes the picaresque novels of the period dull by comparison.

Spain's first woman novelist, María de Zayas (1590–1660), now all but forgotten, expressed distinctly feminist ideas. In prefaces to her *Novelas amorosas exemplares* (1635, 1647) she condemns the double standard, advises women to take pride in their sex, and demands equality of education. Women are far from stupid, but simply "not given the opportunity to apply themselves to study. If in childhood they gave us books and masters instead of lacemaking and embroidery, we would be just as well prepared as men for professorships and positions of state."

There can be no better illustration of this than **Sor Juana Inés de la Cruz** (1648?–1695), who was born and died in Mexico, then a colony of the Spanish Empire called New Spain. A child prodigy who was largely self-educated, she was made part of the Viceroy's entourage in her teens, but in the hope of pursuing her studies in numerous fields she left to become a nun, in a day when convents were the only refuge of artistic and intellectual women. Her thirst for learning, however, brought her into conflict with her ecclesiastical superiors, who advised her to confine her researches to religious matters. Her famous *Reply to Sor Filotea* (1693) defending her right to knowledge, is a major document in the struggle for women's intellectual independence; it was recently published in Barcelona as "The First Women's Manifesto." Sor Juana's poignant awareness of the suppressed potentialities of women makes her the first feminist of the New World and one of its greatest thus far. A few specimens from her large body of work (in all the literary forms of her time) are translated here, including a little-known carol to St. Catherine of Alexandria, a martyr of third-century Egypt and one of the first heroes of feminism, with whom she clearly identified.

Eventually Sor Juana's brilliant voice was silenced; and with the insuperable opposition of the powerful Church-State no other woman's voice even remotely resembling hers was heard in the Hispanic world for more than a century. During the eighteenth and nineteenth centuries, most women were illiterate, even though under Philip V (1701–1746), grandson of Louis XIV of France, Spain underwent a kind of renaissance, with scientists and technicians brought in from abroad, scholarships created for study in France and other European countries, and institutions of learning founded, including the National Library (1711), the Spanish Academy (1714), the Academy of Medicine (1734), and the Academy of History (1738).

This Bourbon period of enlightenment extended through the reigns of Fernando VI (1746–1759) and the intelligent and dynamic Carlos III (1759–1788). An ardent admirer of Father Benito Feijoo (1676–1764), a Galician philosopher and encyclopedist and one of the earliest champions of women's rights in Spain, Carlos III endeavored to attract women to his programs, bringing María Isidra de Guzmán (1768–1805) and the Marchioness of Peñafiel into the Royal Economic Society, amid heated debate. By then, Spain was fiercely divided between a cultured minority who favored importing European modernity, and the *castizos* or conservatives, who clung to the old Spanish ways and, calling these innovators *afrancesados* (Frenchifieds), opposed women participating in national affairs, writing, publishing or even attending the universities and academies. Nevertheless, Josefa Amar (1753–1803) was admitted to the Royal Economic Society of Aragon and published a judicious study of the education of women (1790) as well as a remarkable *Discourse in Defence of Women's Talent and Aptitude for Government and Other Posts Employing Men.* Another defender of women, **Margarita Hickey** (1757–1793), one of the first translators of classical French drama, was a poet who insisted that women who applied themselves surpass men in the sciences as well as the arts.

Controls over free expression by women became tighter during the reign of Carlos IV (1788–1808), inept and reactionary son of Carlos III. Thus María de las Mercedes Gómez Castro's *Portrait of Women's Talent and Character*, though passed by the censor, the famous playwright Leandro Fernández de Moratín, was never published because of a vicar's disapproval (1797). Inés Joyes y Blake's novel *El príncipe de Abisinia*, which exposed men's unfair treatment of women, passed the censor in 1798 only under the pretext that it was a translation from the English. "I cannot abide the ridiculous role which women have to play in this world," reads an appendix to the novel, "now idolized like goddesses, now scorned even by men reputed to be wise. We are loved, hated, praised, vituperated, revered, respected, despised and censored."

Suppression of women's voices continued throughout the nineteenth century, when the country, exhausted after its extensive wars and stunning defeats on land and at sea, remained practically stagnant economically and culturally. In fact, all during the eighteenth and nineteenth centuries Spain assiduously shielded itself from the rationalist ideas of the Enlightenment (prevalent in England, France, Germany, and North America), with its cogent arguments for the rights of man and even, sometimes, the rights of women. Writers like Harriet Martineau, John Stuart Mill, Mary Wollstonecraft, Condorcet, Saint-Simon, Fourier, Mme. de Staël, George Sand, Lessing, the Schlegels, and Margaret Fuller were considered subversive and rigorously excluded.

Not until the latter part of the nineteenth century did Spanish women begin to seek the recognition being gained by other women of Europe. Insisting upon individuality, identity, and a part in political affairs, they demanded above all literacy and education for all women. In Madrid in 1873 a new magazine, *La Ilustración de la Mujer*, published a poem by Ermelinda Ormaeche y Begoña scoffing at the notion that knowledge is harmful to women, and stressing the social importance of educated mothers. Many women, looking beyond the walls of their homes, sought to alleviate intolerable social conditions, especially in the factories and sweatshops endemic to the Industrial Revolution, where women working long hours for low wages suffered mistreatment of all kinds.

Pioneers in this struggle were three outstanding women of Galicia, the remote northwest province often called the Ireland of Spain, whose rebellion in 1846 was ruthlessly put down and its leaders jailed or executed. Concepción Arenal (1820–1893) gained her education by attending the University of Madrid dressed in men's clothing. Internationally known as a sociologist and staunch critic of the inhuman Spanish penal system, she wrote a study of Feijoo as well as numerous books on the condition of women, including *La mujer española*, *La mujer de su casa*, *La condición social de la mujer en España*, and *La mujer del porvenir (The Woman of the Future)*. **Rosalía de Castro** (1837–1885), major poet of nineteenth-century Spain, voiced impassioned sympathy for the downtrodden Galician peasantry and the plight of its women, on whom the burden of poverty fell most heavily and, in her novels, for women who tried to write in a male-controlled literary establishment. Emilia Pardo Bazán (1851–1921), a towering figure in Spanish literature, wrote some fifty books including poetry, fiction, and criticism. The three volumes of *La revolución y la novela en Rusia* (1887) changed the course of the realistic novel in Spain. Notorious for espousing naturalism, considered sordid and immoral, in novels and short stories she unsparingly exposed the squalor, violence, and corruption rampant in Galicia and the rest of Spain.

Though it is rarely emphasized, Pardo Bazán proclaimed herself "a radical feminist." She believed that "every privilege a man has should also belong to women...It is in underdeveloped countries that the woman is considered a beast of burden and sex object. Spanish men make a great pretense of always being preoccupied with the love of women and there can be no greater obstacle than this to the advancement of women. It perpetuates the battle between the sexes which has existed since primitive times." She translated John Stuart Mill's *Subjection of Women* into Spanish, and not only wrote her own study of Feijoo but carried on his work of bringing scientific ideas into Spain with a new encyclopedia modeled after his. In 1916 the University of Madrid created a chair in comparative literature for her (the first in Europe), which she held until her death. Though she hoped for admission to the Spanish Royal Academy, women were excluded until 1979.

In the nineteenth century the long decline of the proud Spanish Empire reached its final stages with the loss of its colonies in the New World, where it left, however, unmistakable traces—not only its language and religion, but its implacable debasement of women. Indeed, in Spanish America women were doubly despised, not only as women, but as members of what the Spaniards regarded as an inferior culture, fit only to be pillaged and destroyed. They had come to America not to settle, but in quest of gold. Even after the original prohibition against marriage with native women gave way, Spanish American women had to contend with male chauvinism rivaled in few areas of the world. Illiterate and for the most part uneducated, treated contemptuously even as wives, they could earn a living only in menial occupations scorned by men: as *tabaqueras* (tobacco workers), *textileras* (textile workers), and seamstresses; some became teachers.

In time, however, in urban centers such as Buenos Aires, Lima, and Santiago de Chile, middle-class women began to devote themselves to the conditions in their countries and to improving the situation of women. The Chilean Rosario Orrego de Uribe wrote a long poem calling for women's education, "La instrucción de la mujer." The Peruvian Clorinda Matto de Turner (1852–1909) edited several journals and wrote provocative novels, notably *Aves sin nido* (1889), depicting the sufferings of the Indians at the hands of landlords and priests. Her compatriot and friend, novelist Mercedes Cabello de Carbonera (1849–1909), was a tireless activist; **Adela Zamudio** (1854–1928) of Bolivia portrayed with compassion and indignation the lot of women in a man's world.

In Spain, however, where to be a feminist meant to be irreligious, feminists suffered hatred, abuse, and even imprisonment; and despite the liberalizing impact of the Generation of 1898 feminism was very slow to develop. "As always, the Spanish women shine for their absence!" remarked a French delegate to an international women's congress in Berlin in 1904. When in 1907 Carmen de Burgos polled the Spanish parliament on women's suffrage, many Republicans and Socialists as well as Conservatives voted against it.

When women finally achieved the vote, during the short-lived Republic of the 1930s, the election in which they voted for the first time saw a Conservative victory, for which the women were blamed, with even the Anarchists declaring women's suffrage "a calamity." Dolores Ibarruri (La Pasionaria) fought back, calling for "a complete renovation of our traditions: the right to work, equitable wages, maternity care, day centers, divorce without preconditions, legalization of abortion." Franco's rise to power seemed to mark the end of all that had been gained, although some women carried the struggle underground. Since 1975 much progress has taken place, as women have flocked to the universities and taken positions in government, industry, publishing, and all the professions. Yet, feminism remains "an empty word in the mind of Spaniards," as Lidia

Falcón noted, as late as 1969, in *Mujer y sociedad*. "Spanish feminism cannot be said to have failed," wrote María Aurelia Capmany in *El feminismo ibérico* (1970), "since it did not even show up on the battlefield."

As for women poets, they faced the almost insuperable task of freeing themselves from the overpowering influence of male poetry, a male-dominated literary structure, and male-imposed definitions of their innate inferiority as *poetisas*. From the last decade of the nineteenth century to the end of World War I, following the French decadents Verlaine, Rimbaud, and Baudelaire, a resurgence of poetry known as Modernism swept through all the countries of the New World, to the point where the mother country was eclipsed and no longer served as model. Spanish American women flooded the presses with their verse, but most could only echo their male exemplars, who tended toward hermetic, dehumanized art. There were, however, exceptions. **Gabriela Mistral** (1889–1957) of Chile, the only Latin American woman to have won the Nobel Prize, was an educator, pacifist, and humanist who wrote with matchless intensity of frustrated and suffering womanhood. Her children's songs and lullabies are among the tenderest in the Spanish language. Without children of her own, she turned her love of children into a universal love for all humanity. She became a kind of world mother, singing about children "as no one before her had ever done," said Paul Valéry. "While so many poets have exalted, celebrated, cursed or invoked death, or built, deepened, divinized the passion of love, few seem to have meditated on that transcendental act par excellence, the production of the living being by the living being."

Delmira Agustini (1886–1914) of Uruguay, probing the essence of female passion and finding an elemental need for an intellectual and spiritual content, rejected purely physical love as incapable of generating the "new breed" she longed for. **Alfonsina Storni** (1892–1938) of Argentina, who with an illegitimate son struggled bitterly and eventually committed suicide, wrote scathing feminist poems. In Mexico **Concha Michel** (b. 1899) is one of the few poets to find inspiration in the ancient culture of the Mayas and its androgynous principle.

The generation of women poets who followed were forced by momentous historical events (World War I, the Russian Revolution, Fascism, the Spanish Civil War) to a more realistic stance, as dramatized in the poetry of the Spaniard **Angela Figuera-Aymerich** (1902–1984), who originally extolled the beauty of her landscape and family life, but after the Civil War turned to "a badly bruised and difficult world [and] the problems and suffering of our times." Known for portraits of downtrodden washerwomen, servant maids, prostitutes, and housewives, she wrote "Destiny," a poignant poem of maternity as enslavement to the species. **Gloria Fuertes** (b. 1918) also lived through the Spanish Civil War, which made her a pacifist, she said, ridiculing with typical Spanish verve the civilization created by men, including bankers, generals, and churchmen. Although her irrepressible wit and fertile, often surrealist fantasy make her seem a humorist in the manner of Ramón Gómez de la Serna, her deep concern is for the human condition, for the disinherited and oppressed: ''I cannot sing of flowers/I sing of men who weep beneath the sun.''Among those who weep she includes women, whose exploiters she calls tigers (''los hombres son tigres''). Like Mistral and Figuera, she treats the problem of maternity in a man's world, but in a lighter vein. We include here a few specimens of her vast production, though her wit is hard to translate because much of it is wordplay, in the long Spanish tradition.

In Spanish America Fuertes's contemporary, **Idea Vilariño** (b. 1920) of Uruguay, was more politically committed. The popular folk songs she wrote for revolutionary singing groups brought her more pleasure, she said, than all her published poetry. Vilariño wrote in an extremely spare, abbreviated style peculiarly her own but suited to her pessimistic message. The brilliant Mexican **Rosario Castellanos** (1925–1974) combines a philosophical outlook with a well-grounded historical perspective in both novels and poems, in which she employs complex striking imagery, as in ''Daily Round of the Spinster,'' another treatment of the theme of the childless woman. A profound student of women's lives, she suggests, as in ''Meditation at the Threshold,'' that the solution, not yet found, requires ''Another way to be human and free./ Another way to be.'' Her powerful utterance opened the way to a new generation of women poets born after 1937, in different countries, but all with a clear apprehension of the contemporary woman's situation; Spain's **Juana Castro** (b. 1948) is among them.

Indeed, if in the Hispanic world feminist poetry was slow to develop, it has blossomed in recent years. Spain has a strong feminist movement in both Madrid and Barcelona, with many women's bookstores and publications, among others the magazine *Urogallo*, featuring the new work of male as well as female writers. In Spanish America women have organized their own societies in every country, as well as a Pan American Congress that meets regularly; they too have their bookshops and periodicals, notably *FEM* of Mexico.

The output of feminist poetry has become so voluminous, the difficulty is to select among such a vast array, all exploring various aspects of women's lives from different points of view. The progression from the anonymous protest at exclusion from the battlefield conveyed in the old ballad ''The Girl Warrior'' is well exemplified in the verse of **Gioconda Belli** (b. 1947), a warrior in the Sandinist revolution in Nicaragua; though most feminist verse today is strongly antimilitary. The Chilean **Raquel Jodorowsky** (b. 1937), for example, writing of nuclear war and the pollution of the earth as special threats to women and children, marvels at ''so much anger in men's mentality'' and their destructiveness, which she feels helpless to combat or relate to in any way. The Argentine **Elena Jordana** (b. 1940) is repelled by today's commercialism and, like **Bessy Reyna**

(b. 1942) of Panama, by men's age-old faithlessness. Some women have sought a solution in love between women—among many others Rosa Chacel, Alejandra Pizarnik, **Cristina Peri Rossi** (b. 1941), and **Pilar Cibreiro**. Others like **Kyra Galván** (b. 1956), view the subordination of women in the context of a large sociopolitical complex, and believe that in their quest for "another way to be" women will require a transformed civilization.

In this anthology we have tried to present the drama of women's struggle for their rights in the Hispanic world, as reflected in its poetry. Spanning almost a thousand years and a dozen countries, this collection lays no claim to being complete, even after years of research. Many of these poems are not part of the Hispanic literary canon. Some have never been anthologized, or even mentioned in histories of Hispanic literature. Moreover names of women not to be ignored—Rosalía de Castro, for example—have seldom been associated with feminism. Others may be alluded to but dismissed as insignificant. Often they are misinterpreted. Delmira Agustini, for example, has been stereotyped as merely a minor love poet in imitation of the Modernists.

Feminism requires a major literary reassessment and reinterpretation—a new feminist criticism. Old molds of thinking will have to be broken, for they were fashioned by men who could not avoid bias if only in the absence of alternative molds. Thus only men could consider Agustini a traditional love poet, although in her rebellion against the carnality of the male concept of love, she may be seen as a revolutionary feminist.

Florencia Pinar is another poet who needs reinterpretation. One of the few women whose names appear in the *Cancioneros*, she has been viewed as a typical "erotic troubadour" of no distinction, Manuel Serrano y Sanz calling her work "quite weak and insubstantial." Recently, however, her "sensual flavor" has been scrutinized, and critics have found considerable merits in her poems. Manuel Alvar praises her "passionate grace and thematic innovations"—traits analyzed in depth by Alan Deyermond and Joseph Snow, both of whom see her theme as "suppressed sexuality." Snow describes her poem about the caged partridges as "veiled eroticism a more fervent expression of which would have been unseemly within the conventions of the courtly lyric." Deyermond speaks of her "strongly sexual tone;" he describes the poem "So wily are the ways of love" as full of phallic and sexual imagery, and suggests she was "tormented by sexual desire." Not only is the worm in this poem a phallic symbol, but the word *natura* possibly "has a second meaning: the sexual organs." She chose partridges as her symbol, Deyermond suggests, because of their extreme sexuality as described in the bestiary, her identification with them thus revealing her sexual torment (even though admittedly there is no Castilian bestiary or evidence she was acquainted with any).

Partridges, however, are known for their singing, and the trapping and caging of singing birds as pets and gifts was a popular pastime among the aristocracy of Pinar's day—"Wasn't that a dainty dish [singing blackbirds baked in a pie] to set before a king?" The first four lines of this poem clearly state the theme: the nature of these birds is to sing in happiness (*con alegría*); to see them imprisoned (and apparently silenced) makes her sad. Her theme, then, is sorrow at their loss of freedom, and it seems at least equally possible that she chose partridges not for their sexual associations but for the verbal associations of their name: in Spanish *perdiz*, partridge, is closely related to *perder*, to lose. One of the charms of this poem is the author's delicate play on these two words, one her central symbol and the other her central theme, *loss*: the partridges' loss of happiness in singing—in freedom, of course—and her own. We see this wordplay and identification with the birds in the climactic ninth and tenth lines: "their names [*perdices*] are my life,/which loses happiness constantly [*va perdiendo alegría*]." Just as they have lost their happiness in freely singing, she is losing hers. For she too is a singer of songs with the same need for freedom to sing. In short, she feels as imprisoned as the partridges, and shares their unhappiness so like her own.

In the fifth line she notes that no one feels her sadness—a line repeated as a refrain concluding the poem, its significance having been clarified in the intervening six lines, which detail her empathy with the partridges. In these lines she does not use the word *perdices* (which is feminine in Spanish), but speaks of "they" in the feminine (*ellas*), while the hunters who caught them (for sport and the admiration of their ladies) are referred to as "*mismos*" (masculine). In thus identifying herself with the partridges she identifies with their captivity as well: she too is a victim of men's urges to conquer and control; men imprison her and muffle her singing just as they have imprisoned the birds and muffled their singing (see also Alfonsina Storni's poem "Small Man").

The repetition of the refrain to the effect that while she grieves for the birds' loss of freedom no one in her world grieves for hers, emphasizes that loss of freedom is the burden of her poem. Indeed it is possible to say that her theme is not the torment of politely suppressed sexual desire, but politely suppressed desire for freedom and her torment at having lost it, apparently irretrievably.

It is a loss of freedom for which she can find no sympathy because her society is oblivious to her need for it. In effect, the poem is a gentle sigh at not only the brutality of trapping and caging birds, but the brutality of the society that finds amusement in the practice. Clearly, where a people are insensitive enough to trap and imprison birds in denial of their birthright of freedom, they are too insensitive to sympathize with a woman's feelings of being trapped and imprisoned, of having lost the freedom that is *her* birthright.

In conventional interpretations of this poem, its irony is lost: the irony of the contrast between freedom and captivity, happiness and grief, singing and silence, and especially the irony of the "gift" of caged birds.

When poems are misunderstood they cannot be properly translated. Every translation is an explication, requiring the translator to choose words and phrases from a range of alternatives having different nuances, and in this choice lies the translator's interpretation.

The aim in this anthology has been faithfulness to meaning, translations that render the statement of the poem as succinctly as the original text.

To this end there has been no effort to retain rhyme schemes, important as these have been in Spanish poetry, especially in its early stage; in the debate-poems of the fifteenth century, for example, one poet would ask a question and another would have to answer in the same rhyme-scheme. To the same end, rhyme is not attempted except where possible without distortion (Spanish is a rhyme-rich language but English is not); or where rhyme is almost a part of the meaning, as in very short poems or some of the old ballads. Sometimes half-rhyme is used to suggest full rhyme in the original, as is alliteration. Wordplay, beloved of Spanish poets, has had to be sacrificed in almost all instances. Thus, in the poem "My Parents, as if Enemies" by the Nun of Alcalá, *grada* (the convent grate through which inmates had to converse with visitors) is contrasted with *agrado*, or pleasure.

There has, however, been some attempt at rhythm, even if not necessarily the rhythm of the Spanish original, since without rhythm, translations (even if rhymed and rhyme-schemed) are merely prose, and often not very good prose.

No translations have been taken from the anthologies of others, and nearly all have been made specifically for this volume. Indeed, some poems have never existed in English translation, the originals having been found in old forgotten works, or submitted by poets themselves, some in manuscript. We wish to thank all those poets, and to express our regret to those we have had to forego not for reasons of merit but of space. While we have tried to represent as many Spanish-speaking countries as possible, we have made no attempt to include the many fine Catalan women poets—Maria-Mercè Marçal, Marta Pessarrodona, Mari Chordà, Maria Strúmbol, Tat Fortuny, and Rosa Fabregat, to mention a few.

Many people contributed to the preparation of this book. It is a pleasure to record our gratitude for the unfailing assistance of Ruth Hollander, Isabella Taler, and Rochelle Winchel of the Interlibrary Loan Department of the Paul Klapper Library, Queens College, as well as to friends, colleagues and former students who have helped in various ways: Ronald Cere, literary critic and historian; the historian Jean Christie; Lisa E. Davis; Juan Flores (Queens College); the Mexican poet Isabel Fraire; Rubén González (State University of New York, Old Westbury); Yanis Gordils (Hunter College); Norma Klahn (Columbia University); and the Chilean poet and artist Cecilia Vicuña. Joanne O'Hare of The Feminist Press made numerous helpful suggestions.

The Defiant Muse

HISPANIC FEMINIST POEMS FROM THE MIDDLE AGES TO THE PRESENT

LA NIÑA GUERRERA

Estaba un buen día un viejo
sentado en un campo al sol.
—Pregonadas son las guerras
de Francia con Aragón...
¿Cómo las haré yo, triste
viejo, cano y pecador?—

De allí fué para su casa
echando una maldición.
—¡Reventarás tú, María,
por medio del corazón;
que pariste siete hijas
y entre ellas ningún varón!—

La más chiquita de ellas
salió con buena razón:
—No la maldigáis, mi padre,
no la maldigáis, non;
que yo iré a servir al rey
en hábitos de varón.
Compraráisme vos, mi padre,
calcetas y buen jubón;
daréisme las vuestras armas,
vuestro caballo trotón.
—Conoceránte en los ojos,
hija, que muy bellos son.
—Yo los bajaré a la tierra
cuando pase algún varón.
—Conoceránte en los pechos,
que asoman por el jubón.
—Esconderélos, mi padre;
al par de mi corazón.
—Conoceránte en los pies,
que muy menuditos son.
—Pondréme las vuestras botas
bien rellenas de algodón...
¿Cómo me he de llamar, padre,
cómo me he de llamar yo?
—Don Martinos, hija mía,
que así me llamaba yo—

ANONYMOUS BALLADS AND SONGS
(SPAIN, THIRTEENTH–SIXTEENTH CENTURIES)

THE GIRL WARRIOR

One fine day an old man
was sitting outdoors in the sun.
—"Town criers have proclaimed
war between France and Aragon...
What am I, old gray-haired sinner,
to do?"

And so he went indoors
uttering cries.
—"Curse you, María,
may your heart crack in halves,
for having given birth to seven girls
and not a single boy!"

The youngest of the girls
arose in her mother's defense:
—"Don't curse her, father dear,
curse her not,
for dressed as a boy
I shall go to serve the King.
Buy for me
hose and a goodly doublet;
pass on to me your weapons
and your trotting horse."
—"They will detect you for your eyes,
they are so beautiful, daughter!"
—"I shall lower them
whenever a man goes by."
—"They will detect you for your breasts
protruding from your doublet."
—"I shall hide them, father,
close against my heart."
—"They will detect you for your feet,
which are so tiny."
—"I shall wear your boots
properly stuffed with cotton...
What shall my name be, father,
What shall I call myself?"
—"Don Martinos, my daughter,
for that was my name."

Yera en palacio del rey,
y nadie la conoció,
si no es el hijo del rey,
que della se enamoró.
—Tal caballero, mi madre,
doncella me pareció.
—¿En qué lo conocéis, hijo;
en qué lo conocéis vos?
—En poner el su sombrero
y en abrochar el jubón,
y en poner de las calcetas,
¡mi Dios, como ella las pon!
—Brindaréisla vos, mi hijo,
para en las tierras mercar;
si el caballero era hembra,
corales querrá llevar—.
El caballero es discreto
y un puñal tomó en la man.
—Los ojos de don Martinos
roban el alma al mirar.
—Brindaréisla vos, mi hijo.
al par de vos acostar;
si el caballero era hembra,
tal convite non quedrá—.
El caballero es discreto
y echóse sin desnudar.
—Los ojos de don Martinos
roban el alma al mirar.
—Brindaréisla vos, mi hijo,
a dir con vos a la mar.
Si el caballero era hembra,
él se habrá de acobardar—.

El caballero es discreto,
luego empezara a llorar.
—¿Tú qué tienes, don Martinos,
que te pones a llorar?
—Que se me ha muerto mi padre,
y mi madre en eso va;
si me dieran la licencia
fuérala yo a visitar.
—Esa licencia, Martinos,
de tuyo la tienes ya.
Ensilla un caballo blanco,
y en él luego ve a montar—.

And so she arrived at the King's palace,
and no one detected her
no one but the King's son,
who fell in love with her.
—"That gentleman, mother,
seems to be a girl."
—"How did you detect it, son,
how did you detect it?"
—"By the way she wears her hat,
and the way she clasps her doublet,
and the way she puts on her hose,
my God, how she puts them on!"
—"Invite her then, my son,
to go shopping with you;
if the gentleman is a female
she will want to buy corals.
A gentleman is discreet,
and will buy only a dagger."
—"With her glances Don Martinos' eyes
steal away my soul!"
—"Invite her then, my son,
to lie down close beside you,
if the gentleman is female
she will not accept the invitation.
A gentleman is discreet
and lies down without undressing."
—"With her glances Don Martinos' eyes
steal away my soul!"
—"Invite her then, my son,
to go with you to the sea.
If the gentleman is female
she will be afraid."

The gentleman is discreet
and breaks out into tears.
—"What's wrong with you, Don Martinos,
why do you weep?"
—"It's because my father has died,
and my mother is busy with this;
if they give me a furlough
I shall go to visit her."
—"That furlough, Martinos,
is granted to you right now.
Saddle a white horse
and set off right away."

Por unas vegas arriba
corre como un gavilán,
por otras vegas abajo
corre sin le divisar.
—Adiós, adiós, el buen rey,
y su palacio real;
que siete años le serví
doncella de Portugal,
y otros siete le sirviera
si non fuese el desnudar—.

Oyólo el hijo del rey,
de altas torres donde está;
reventó siete caballos
para poderla alcanzar.
Allegando ella su casa,
todos la van a abrazar.
Pidió la rueca a su madre
a ver si sabía filar.
—Deja la rueca, Martinos,
non te pongas a filar;
que si de la guerra vienes,
a la guerra has de tornar.
Ya están aquí tus amores,
los que te quieren llevar.

NO QUERADES, FIJA

No querades, fija,
marido tomar,
para sospirar.

Fuese mi marido
a la frontera;
sola me deja
en tierra ajena.

No querades, fija,
marido tomar,
para sospirar.

Up across the farmlands
he rides on like a hawk,
and down across the farmlands
so fast does he ride you can hardly see him.
—"Goodbye, good King, goodbye,
royal palace;
for seven years
a maid from Portugal
has served him,
and for seven more would I serve him
provided I didn't have to undress."

The King's son heard this
from the high tower where he stood;
he wore out seven horses
in trying to overtake her.
As she approached her home,
everyone came out to greet her.
She asked her mother for a distaff
to see if she knew how to spin.
—"Put the distaff aside, Martinos,
you do not need to spin,
for if you come from the battlefield
to the battlefield you must return.
Here is your love
come to take you away."

—*Ángel Flores*

DO NOT, DAUGHTER

Do not, daughter,
for a husband try,
'tis but to sigh.

To the front
my husband's gone;
in a foreign land
he's left me alone.

Do not, daughter,
for a husband try,
'tis but to sigh.

—*Kate Flores*

SILVANA SE VA A PASEAR

Silvana se va a pasear
por su corredor arriba,
si bien canta, mejor baila
mejor romances decía;
y su padre la miraba
por un mirador que había.
—¡Qué bien te está, hija Silvana,
la ropa de cada día!
Mejor tu madre la reina,
vestida de peregrina. —
Porque Silvana no quiere
sin agua la encierra viva.
Al otro día siguiente
se asoma por la ventana,
y ve a sus dos hermanitos
jugando juego de espadas.
—Por Dios le pido a mi hermano
que me traiga un vaso de agua,
que antes de morir de sed,
a Dios quiero dar mi alma.

AGORA QUE SOY NIÑA

Agora que soy niña
   quiero alegría,
que no se sirve Dios
   de mi monjía.

Agora que soy niña,
   niña en cabello,*
¿me queréis meter monja
   en el monesterio?
¡Que no se sirve Dios
   de mi monjía!

Agora que soy niña
   quiero alegría,
que no se sirve Dios
   de mi monjía.

*In medieval Spain, *niña en cabello* meant an adolescent girl.

SILVANA GOES A-STROLLING*

Silvana goes a-strolling
along her upstairs hall.
If she sings well, she dances better,
reciting ballads best of all.
From a lookout point her father
keeps his eye affixed upon her.
"Daughter Silvana, how well you look
in your everyday attire—
better than the queen your mother
decked out in all her finery."
Because Silvana does not care to,
she is imprisoned without water.
One day looking out a window
she spies her two small brothers
playing at dueling one another.
"For God's sake I beg of you, my brother,
bring to me a glass of water,
for before I die of thirst
my soul to God I would give first."

—*Kate Flores*

NOW THAT I'M YOUNG

Now that I'm young
  I want my fun,
I can't serve God
  being a nun.

Now that I'm young
  and come of age,
why be a nun
  in a convent caged?
I can't serve God
  being a nun!

Now that I'm young
  I want my fun,
I can't serve God
  being a nun.

—*William M. Davis*

*Rondelay still sung in Matanzas, Cuba, end of the nineteenth century.

DESDE NIÑA ME CASARON

Desde niña me casaron
por amores que no amé:
mal casadita me llamaré.

DELGADINA

El buen rey tenía tres hijas
muy hermosas y galanas,
la más chiquita dellas
Delgadina se llamaba.
—Delgadina de cintura,
tú has de ser mi enamorada.
—No lo quiera Dios del cielo
ni la Virgen soberana
que yo enamorada fuera
del padre que me engendrara—.
El padre, que tal oyó,
la encerrara en una sala.
Non le daban de comer
más que de carne salada;
non la daban de beber,
sino zumo de naranja.
A la mañana otro día
se asomara a la ventana
y viera a su madre en bajo
en silla de oro sentada:
—¡Mi madre, por ser mi madre
púrrame una jarra d' agua,
porque me muero de sede
y a Dios quiero dar el alma!
—Calla tú, perra maldita,
calla tú, perra malvada;
siete años que estoy contigo,
siete años soy mal casada—.
A la mañana otro día
se asomara a otra ventana;
vió a sus hermanas en bajo,
filando seda labrada.
—¡Hermanas, las mis hermanas,
purrírme una jarra d' agua,

WHEN I WAS A CHILD THEY MARRIED ME

When I was a child they married me:
Now I'm ill wedded,
a baby ill bedded.

—*Kate Flores*

DELGADINA

The good king had three daughters,
All graceful and all fair,
The youngest was Delgadina.
"Now come, my Delgadina,
For you must lie with me."
"Neither the Lord of Heaven
Nor our most sovereign Lady
Wishes that I should lie
With the father who begot me."
Her father in his anger
Locked her into a room
With nothing for her hunger
But a little salted meat,
With nothing for her thirst
But the drip of a green orange.
When it was morning she looked
Out of a high window,
Down in the garden her mother
Sat in a golden chair.
"My mother, because you are
My mother, bring me water,
I am dying of thirst, I want
To give up my soul to God."
"Be quiet, bitch of a daughter,
Be quiet, you are to blame
That for seven years I have known
The shame of a bad marriage."
On the next morning she looked
From another high window,
Down in the yard her sisters
Were spinning out the silk.
"My sisters, because you are
My sisters, bring me water,
I am dying of thirst, I want

que ya me muero de sede
y, a Dios quiero dar el alma!
—Primero te meteríamos
esta encina por la cara—.
Se asomara al otro día
a otra ventana más alta;
vió a sus hermanos que en bajo
taban tirando la barra:
—¡Hermanos, por ser hermanos,
purrírme una jarra d' agua,
que ya me muero de sede
y a Dios quiero dar mi alma!
—Non te la doy, Delgadina;
non te la damos, Delgada,
que si tu padre lo sabe
nuestra vida es ya juzgada—.
Se asomara al otro día
a otra ventana más alta,
y vió a su padre que en bajo
paseaba en una sala:
—¡Mi padre, por ser mi padre,
púrrame una jarra d' agua,
porque me muero de sede
y a Dios quiero dar el alma!
—Darétela, Delgadina,
si me cumples la palabra.
—La palabra cumpliréla,
aunque sea de mala gana.
—Acorred, mis pajecicos,
a Delgadina con agua;
el primero que llegase
con Delgadina se casa;
el que llegare postrero
su vida será juzgada—
Unos van con jarros de oro,
otros con jarros de plata...
Las campanas de la iglesia
por Delgadina tocaban.
El primero que llegó,
Delgadina era finada.
La cama de Delgadina
de ángeles está cercada;
bajan a la de su padre,
de demonios coronada.

To give my soul to God."
"If only we had a knife
We would throw it in your face."
On the next morning she looked
From another high window,
Down in the court her brothers
Were practicing with their spears.
"My brothers, because you are
My brothers, bring me water,
I am dying of thirst, I want
To give up my soul to God."
"No, Delgadina, no,
We cannot bring you water,
For if your father knew,
Our punishment would be death."
On the next morning she looked
From another window,
Down in the hall her father
Was pacing to and fro.
"My father, because you are
My father, bring me water,
I am dying of thirst, I want
To give up my soul to God."
"Yes, I will bring you water
If you will do as I wish."
"Yes, I will do as you wish."
"Now run, my pageboys, run,
Bring water to Delgadina:
The first of you to arrive
Shall have her hand in marriage,
The last to arrive shall die."
Some ran with silver pitchers,
Some with pitchers of gold...
While the church bells were ringing
For Delgadina's soul.
When the first page arrived,
He found that she was dead,
Around her bed a ring
Of blessed angels stood,
The bed of the king her father
Was crowned with a ring of fiends.

—Lysander Kemp

SER QUIERO, MADRE

Ser quiero, madre,
señora de mí,
no quiero ver
mal gozo de mí.

Dize mi madre
que me meta monja,
que me dará frayle
cual yo lo excoxa;

mas bien entiendo
la su lisonja;
no verá çierto
tal gozo de mí.

DE SER MALCASADA

De ser malcasada
no lo niego yo,
cativo se vea
quien me cativó.

Cativo se vea
y sin redençión;
dolor y pasión
con él siempre sea;
su mal no se vea
pues el mío no vió;
cativo se vea
quien me cativó.

Yo, triste cuitada,
la muerte deseo
y nunca la veo,
que soy desdichada.

Tan triste casada
ya nunca se vió.
Cativo se vea
quien me cativó.

Mugeres casadas
que tal padecéis:

I WANT TO BE, MOTHER

I want to be, mother,
wife to whom I choose,
I do not wish to see
my favors ill used.

A nun my mother wishes
that I be,
she will get me a friar,
any one I desire;

but I know all too well
what it is she offers me;
never will she see
such favors from me.

—*Kate Flores*

THAT I'M ILL MARRIED

That I'm ill married
I can't deny:
May my jailer feel
As jailed as I.

May he feel jailed
And thrown away;
May pain and suffering
Dog his day.
May trouble see him;
May his luck be blind.
May my jailer feel
As jailed as I.

How hopelessly
For death I pine,
But death is deaf
To my luckless sigh.

A sadder wife
You'll never find.
May my jailer feel
As jailed as I.

Married women
Who suffer this,

si vida tenéis
sois muy desdichadas:
seréis lastimadas
si sois como yo.
Cativo se vea
quien me cativó.

¿PARA QUÉ QUIERO CASARME?

¿Para qué quiero casarme
si el marido ha de mandarme?

ELL AMOR HA TALES MAÑAS

Ell amor ha tales mañas,
que quien no se guarda dellas,
si se le entra en las entrañas,
no puede salir sin ellas.

Ell amor es vn gusano,
bien mirada su figura;
es vn cancer de natura
que como todo lo sano:
por sus burlas, por sus sañas,
del se dan tales querellas,
que si entra en las entrañas,
no puede salir sin ellas.

If you're alive
You're in distress:
Your hide's been hit
The same as mine.
May my jailer feel
As jailed as I.

—*William M. Davis*

WHY SHOULD I BE WITH A HUSBAND BOUND?

Why should I be with a husband bound
who merely orders me around?

—*Kate Flores*

FLORENCIA PINAR
(Spain, c. 1460)

SO WILY ARE THE WAYS OF LOVE

So wily are the ways of love,
that one must always be on guard,
for if it enters within the entrails,
without them it will not depart.

Love, rightly seen,
has the shape of a worm;
'tis a cancer of nature,
all things healthy consuming:
with its trickeries, with its deceits,
squabbles without end it starts,
for if it enters within the entrails,
without them it will not depart.

—*Kate Flores*

A UNAS PERDICES QUE LE ENVIARON VIVAS

Destas aues su nacion
es cantar con alegria,
y de vellas en prission
siento yo graue passion,
sin sentir nadie la mia.

Ellas lloran que se vieron
sin temor de ser catiuas,
y a quien eran mas esquiuas
essos mismos las prendieron:
sus nombres mi vida son
que va perdiendo alegria,
y de vellas en prission
siento yo graue passion,
sin sentir nadie la mia.

DÉCIMAS ESCRITAS MUY DE PRIESSA,
EN RESPUESTA DE OTRAS EN QUE PONDERABAN
LA MUDANZA DE LAS MUJERES

Hombres, no desonoréis
con título de inconstantes
las mujeres, que diamantes
son, si obligarlas sabéis.
Si alguna mudable veis,
la mudanza es argumento
de que antes quiso de asiento...
Si mujer dice mudanza
el hombre mentira dice...
si se ajusta á igual balanza
por la cuenta se hallaría
en él mentir cada día
y en mudarse cada mes,
que el mentir vileza es;
mudar de hombres, mejoría.

ON SOME PARTRIDGES SENT TO HER ALIVE

The nature of these birds
is with happiness to sing,
and to see them imprisoned
sadness to me brings,
sadness no one seems to share.

They weep to reflect
that they never feared capture,
and that those they most eluded
are the ones who entrapped them:
their names are my life,
which loses happiness constantly,
and to see them imprisoned
brings sadness to me,
sadness no one seems to share.

—*Kate Flores*

MARCIA BELISARDA
(SPAIN, ?–1647)

STANZAS WRITTEN IN GREAT HASTE IN REPLY
TO SOME PROPOSING THAT WOMEN ARE FICKLE

Men, do not dishonor
women by calling them fickle
for they are diamonds
if you know how to treat them.
If you find one who seems inconstant
her inconstancy proves
she was seeking after permanence...
If a man says women are fickle
he utters a lie...
Were the scales to be balanced
it would be reckoned
that he lies every day
and changes each month;
since lying is vileness
'twere better men be changed.

—*Kate Flores*

ARGUYE DE INCONSECUENTES EL GUSTO Y LA CENSURA DE LOS HOMBRES QUE EN LAS MUJERES ACUSAN LO QUE CAUSAN

Hombres necios que acusáis
A la mujer, sin razón,
Sin ver que sois la ocasión
De lo mismo que culpáis:

Si con ansia sin igual
Solicitáis su desdén
¿Por qué queréis que obren bien,
Si las incitáis al mal?

Combatís su resistencia,
Y luego, con gravedad,
Decís que fué liviandad
Lo que hizo la diligencia.

Queréis, con presunción necia,
Hallar á la que buscáis,
Para pretendida, Thais,
Y en la posesión, Lucrecia.

Opinión, ninguna gana;
Pues la que más se recata,
Si no os admite, es ingrata,
Y si os admite, es liviana.

Siempre tan necios andáis,
Que, con desigual nivel,
A una culpáis por cruel,
Y á otra por fácil culpáis.

Dan vuestras amantes penas
A sus libertades alas,
Y después de hacerlas malas,
Las quereis hallar muy buenas.

¿Cuál mayor culpa ha tenido
En una pasión errada:
La que cae de rogada,
O el que ruega de caído?

SOR JUANA INÉS DE LA CRUZ
(MEXICO, 1648?–1695)

ARGUING THAT THERE ARE INCONSISTENCIES BETWEEN
MEN'S TASTES AND THEIR CENSURE WHEN THEY ACCUSE
WOMEN OF WHAT THEY THEMSELVES DO CAUSE

You foolish men, who accuse
Women without good reason,
You are the cause of what you blame,
Yours the guilt you deny.

If you seek the love of women to win
With ardor beyond compare,
Why require them to be good,
When 'tis you who urge their sin?

You break down their resistance,
Then declare quite seriously
That their lightness has achieved
What you won by your persistence.

You seek with stupid presumption
To find her whom you pursue
To be Thaïs when you woo her,
And Lucretia in your possession.

No woman can you really win
Since even the most discreet
Is ungrateful if she keeps you out
And loose if she lets you in.

So where is the woman born
Who would gain your love,
If an ungrateful woman displeases
And a complaisant one you scorn?

Your amorous labors give
Wings to their indiscretions,
When you have made women wicked
You wish them virtuously to live.

In a passion that is guilty
Who bears the greater blame:
She who falls on being entreated
Or he who falls to make entreaty?

¿O cuál es más de culpar,
Aunque cualquiera mal haga:
La que peca por la paga,
O el que paga por pecar?

¿Pues para qué os espantáis
De la culpa que tenéis?
Queredlas cual las hacéis,
O hacedlas cual las buscáis.

Dejad de solicitar,
Y después, con más razón,
Acusaréis la afición
De la que os fuere á rogar.

Bien con muchas armas fundo
Que lidia vuestra arrogancia,
Pues en promesa e instancia
Juntáis diablo, carne y mundo.

A SU RETRATO

Este que ves, engaño colorido,
que, del arte ostentando los primores,
con falsos silogismos de colores
es cauteloso engaño del sentido;

éste, en quien la lisonja ha pretendido
excusar de los años los horrores,
y venciendo del tiempo los rigores
triunfar de la vejez y del olvido,

es un vano artificio del cuidado,
es una flor al viento delicada,
es un resguardo inútil para el hado:

es una necia diligencia errada,
es un afán caduco y, bien mirado,
es cadáver, es polvo, es sombra, es nada.

When each is guilty of sin,
Which is the most to blame:
She who sins for payment,
Or he who pays for the sin?

Why are you so surprised
At the fault that is your own?
Either prize women as you make them,
Or make them to be prized.

To them no longer urge your suit,
And then with much more reason
Can you blame their affection
When they are in pursuit.

To assert this I have every right;
Your pride has many weapons,
Your persistence and your promises
Devil, world, and flesh unite.

—*Muriel Kittel*

ON HER PORTRAIT

What here you see, in beguiling tints,
Flaunting its cunning artifice
In specious syllogisms of color,
Is a clever deception of the senses;

This, which flattery would fain pretend
Could expiate the horrors of the years,
The ravages of time obliterate
To triumph over age and oblivion,

Is against fate a futile artifact,
Is but a fragile flower in the wind,
Is against time an unavailing foil:

Is merely a folly elaborately in error,
Is merely a senile ardor and, truly seen,
Is skeleton, is dust, is shadow, is nothing.

—*Kate Flores*

VILLANCICO A CATARINA

ESTRIBILLO
¡Víctor, víctor Catarina,
que con su ciencia divina
los sabios ha convencido,
y victoriosa ha salido
—con su ciencia soberana—
de la arrogancia profana
que a convencerla ha venido!
¡Víctor, víctor, víctor!

COPLAS
De una Mujer se convencen
todos los Sabios de Egipto,
para prueba de que el sexo
no es esencia en lo entendido.
¡Víctor, víctor!

Prodigio fué, y aun milagro;
pero no estuvo el prodigio
en vencerlos, sino en que
ellos se den por vencidos.
¡Víctor, víctor!

¡Qué bien se ve que eran Sabios
en confesarse rendidos,
que es triunfo el obedecer
de la razón el dominio!
¡Víctor, víctor!...

No se avergüenzan los Sabios
de mirarse convencidos;
porque saben, como Sabios,
que su saber es finito.
¡Víctor, víctor!

Estudia, arguye y enseña,
y es de la Iglesia servicio,
que no la quiere ignorante
El que racional la hizo.
¡Víctor, víctor!

¡Oh qué soberbios vendrían,
al juntarlos Maximino!
Mas salieron admirados
los que entraron presumidos,
¡Víctor, víctor!

CAROL TO CATHERINE

REFRAIN
Hallelujah, hallelujah, Catherine,
you who with divine science
convinced the sages,
emerging triumphant
—thanks to your amazing wisdom—
over the profane arrogance
attempting to vanquish you!
Hallelujah, hallelujah, hallelujah!

SONG
One woman convinced
all the sages of Egypt
that to be female does not mean to lack wisdom.
Hallelujah, hallelujah!

It was a feat, a miracle even;
yet the feat was not
to have overcome them, but for them
to have conceded defeat.
Hallelujah, hallelujah!

How clear it is they were wise men,
when they conceded their defeat,
for it is an achievement to have bowed
to the supremacy of reason!
Hallelujah, hallelujah!...

The sages were not ashamed
to find themselves convinced;
for they knew, being wise men,
that their knowledge was not infinite.
Hallelujah, hallelujah!

She studied, taught and argued,
and thereby served the Church,
for He who created her a rational being
did not want her ignorant.
Hallelujah, hallelujah!

Oh, how proudly they must have come
when Maximinus convened them!
But they returned chastened,
who had come so vainglorious.
Hallelujah, hallelujah!

Vencidos, con ella todos
la vida dan al cuchillo:
¡oh cuánto bien se perdiera
si Docta no hubiera sido!
¡Víctor, víctor!

Nunca de varón ilustre
triunfo igual habemos visto;
y es que quiso Dios en ella
honrar el sexo femíneo.
¡Víctor, víctor!

Ocho y diez vueltas del Sol,
era el espacio florido
de su edad; mas de su ciencia
¿quién podrá contar los siglos?
¡Víctor, víctor!

Perdióse (¡oh dolor!) la forma
de sus doctos silogismos:
pero, los que no con tinta,
dejó con su sangre escritos.
¡Víctor, víctor!

Tutelar sacra Patrona,
es de las Letras Asilo;
porque siempre ilustre Sabios,
quien Santos de Sabios hizo.
¡Víctor, víctor!

EN PERSEGUIRME, MUNDO, ¿QUÉ INTERESAS?

En perseguirme, Mundo, ¿qué interesas?
¿En qué te ofendo, cuando sólo intento
poner bellezas en mi entendimiento
y no mi entendimiento en las bellezas?

Yo no estimo tesoros ni riquezas;
y así, siempre me causa más contento
poner riquezas en mi pensamiento
que no mi pensamiento en las riquezas.

She, and all of them,
conquered, were put to death:
Oh, what goodness would have been lost
had she been less learned!
Hallelujah, hallelujah!

Never has a man
achieved a triumph so illustrious;
and it was because God wished
to honor through her the female sex.
Hallelujah, hallelujah!

Eight and ten turns of the sun
was the blossoming space
of her age; but as for her wisdom,
who can count the centuries?
Hallelujah, hallelujah!

Alas! the form
of her wise syllogisms has been lost:
but though with ink she did not pen them,
she left them signed with her blood.
Hallelujah, hallelujah!

Sacred tutelary Patroness,
she is the Asylum of Literature;
may she always inspire sages,
she who of sages made saints.
Hallelujah, hallelujah!

—*Kate Flores*

WHAT INTEREST HAVE YOU, WORLD, IN PERSECUTING ME?

What interest have you, world, in persecuting me?
Wherein do I offend you, when all I want
Is to give beauty to my mind
And not my mind to beautiful things?

I do not care for goods or treasures;
And so am always more content
To endow my thoughts with riches
Rather than riches with my thoughts.

Y no estimo hermosura que, vencida,
es despojo civil de las edades,
ni riqueza me agrada fementida,

teniendo por mejor, en mis verdades,
consumir vanidades de la vida
que consumir la vida en vanidades.

MIS PADRES, COMO ENEMIGOS

Mis padres, como enemigos
de la vida que me han dado,
en vida me han sepultado
entre hierros y postigos...

Solo en tanto sentir siento
que más vale, aunque fingido,
un agrado de un marido
que una grada de convento.

And I esteem not looks, which age
Takes away in civil stealth,
Nor am I impressed by wealth,

Holding that in truth 'tis better
To expend the vanities of life
Than to expend one's life in vanities.

—*Kate Flores*

A NUN FROM ALCALÁ
(SPAIN, LATE SEVENTEENTH CENTURY)

MY PARENTS, AS IF ENEMIES

My parents, as if enemies
of the life they gave me,
alive have buried me here
between wickets and iron bars...

Where all that I can feel
is that a pleasing mate,
even if imaginary,
is more pleasing than a convent grate.

—*Kate Flores*

EL VERDADERO SABIO

Que el verdadero sabio, donde quiera
Que la verdad y la razón encuentre,
Allí sabe tomarla, y la aprovecha
Sin nimio detenerse en quién la ofrece.
Porque ignorar no puede, si es que sabe,
Que el alma, como espíritu, carece
De sexo...
Pues cada dia, instantes y momentos,
Vemos aventajarse las mujeres
En las artes y ciencias á los hombres,
Si con aplicación su estudio emprenden.

DE BIENES DESTITUIDAS

De bienes destituidas,
Víctimas del pundonor,
Censuradas con amor,
Y sin él desatendidas;
Sin cariño pretendidas,
Por apetito buscadas,
Conseguidas, ultrajadas;
Sin aplausos la virtud,
Sin lauros la juventud,
Y en la vejez despreciadas.

MARGARITA HICKEY
(SPAIN, 1753–c.1791)

THE TRULY WISE MAN

The truly wise man, whercsoever
He may find truth and reason,
Knows how to embrace it and make use of it,
Without delaying to find out by whom it is offered.
For he cannot ignore, if he is truly wise,
That the soul, being spirit,
Is lacking in sex...
For each day, each hour, each minute,
We see women in the arts and sciences
Surpassing men,
When they apply themselves to their study.

—*Kate Flores*

OF PROPERTY NAUGHT

Of property naught,
Victims of dishonor,
In love criticized,
And without it despised;
Without affection courted,
Out of desire sought,
Conquered, insulted;
Virtue unapplauded,
Youth unrewarded,
And in age discarded.

—*Kate Flores*

de RESOLUCIÓN

¿Que yo escriba? No por cierto,
no me dé Dios tal manía;
ántes una pulmonía,
primero irme á un desierto.

Antes que componer, quiero
tener por esposo un rudo,
mal nacido, testarudo,
avariento y pendenciero...

Si yo compongo, mi rima
censure el dómine necio,
lea el sabio con desprecio,
y un zafio cajista imprima;

Un muchacho la recite
con monotona cadencia,
la destroce en mi presencia,
y ponga frases y quite...

¡Oh! No habrá quien me convenza,
bien puede usted argüir:
¡una mujer escribir
en España! ¡Qué vergüenza!

¿Pues no se viera en mal hora
que la necia bachillera
hasta francés aprendiera?
¿Ha de ir de embajadora?

Antes, señor, las muchachas
no estudiaban, ni leian...
pero en cambio, ¡cuál fregaban!
¡Barrian con un primor!

Hilaban como la araña,
amasaban pan, cernían,
y apuesto que no sabían
si el godo invadió ó no España.

¿Que lo importa á la mujer
de dó se exporta el cacao,

JOSEFA MASANÉS
(SPAIN, 1811–1887)

from RESOLUTION

That I be a writer? Absolutely not!
God spare me such a mania;
rather pneumonia;
I'd go off to the wilderness first.

Rather than writing poems I'd prefer
a roughneck husband,
ill-bred, bullheaded,
miserly and quarrelsome...

Were I to write, my verses
would be censured by some idiot teacher,
read with scorn by the learned,
put together by some illiterate typesetter;

A schoolboy would recite them
with monotonous cadence,
destroy them in my presence
by adding or omitting phrases...

Oh! Nobody could convince me,
for well you could argue:
a woman writing
in Spain! What a disgrace!

Will not next come the evil hour
when the foolish girl
will be learning French?
even be going off as Ambassador?

In the good old days, señor, girls
did not study, or read...
but on the other hand, how they scrubbed!
How beautifully they swept!

They used to spin like spiders;
they kneaded bread, they baked;
and one thing is sure, they had no idea
whether the Goths invaded Spain or not.

What does it matter if a woman
knows where cacao comes from,

si es pesca ó no el bacalao,
como lo sepa cocer?

¡Cuál quedara mi persona,
mordida por tanta boca!
Me llamaran necia, loca,
visionaria, doctorona.

Sin amor ni compasión,
alguno, con tono ambiguo,
dice que de escrito antiguo
es copia mi concepción.

Sin aseo la loquilla,
siempre á vueltas con Cervántes,
recitando consonantes
de Calderón ó Zorrilla,

¿Cómo podrá gobernar
bien su casa? ¡Es imposible!
¡Cual si fuera incompatible
coser y raciocinar.

Anatema al escribir,
al meditar y leer;
amigo, sólo coser
y murmurar, ó dormir.

whether bacalao is a fish or not
so long as she knows how to cook it?...

What would be left of me, señor,
bitten by so many mouths!
They would call me silly, insane,
visionary, pretentious.

Without love or compassion
someone, in no uncertain terms,
would say that from some old book
I had copied my idea...

"The dirty slut
always fussing about Cervantes,
reciting rhymes
of Calderón or Zorrilla,

How can she take care
of her house? It's impossible!"
As if sewing and thinking
were incompatible!...

Down with writing,
down with thinking and reading;
just sew, my friend,
and gossip, or sleep.

—Robert L. Smith and Judith Candullo

QUEJAS

¡Y amarle pude! Al sol de la existencia
se abría apenas soñadora el alma...
Perdió mi pobre corazón su calma
desde el fatal instante en que le hallé.
Sus palabras sonaron en mi oído
como música blanda y deliciosa;
subió a mi rostro el tinte de la rosa;
como la hoja en el árbol vacilé.

Su imagen en el sueño me acosaba
siempre halagüeña, siempre enamorada:
mil veces sorprendiste, madre amada,
en mi boca un suspiro abrasador;
y era él quien lo arrancaba de mi pecho;
él, la fascinación de mis sentidos;
él, ideal de mis sueños más queridos;
él, mi primero, mi ferviente amor.

Sin él, para mí el campo placentero
en vez de flores me obsequiaba abrojos;
sin él eran sombríos a mis ojos
del sol los rayos en el mes de abril.
Vivía de su vida apasionada;
era el centro de mi alma el amor suyo;
era mi aspiración, era mi orgullo...
¿Por qué tan presto me olvidaba el vil?

No es mío ya su amor, que a otra prefiere.
Sus caricias son frías como el hielo;
es mentira su fe, finge desvelo...
Mas no me engañará con su ficción...
¡Y amarle pude, delirante, loca!
¡No, mi altivez no sufre su maltrato!
Y si a olvidar no alcanzas al ingrato,
¡te arrancaré del pecho, corazón!

DOLORES VEINTIMILLA DE GALINDO
(ECUADOR, 1830–1857)

LAMENTS

Oh I could love him! My dreaming soul
Just opening to the sun of existence...
My poor heart lost its serenity
From the fatal moment I found him.
His words sounded in my ear
Like soft and delectable music.
A tint of rose came into my face
And I trembled like a leaf on a tree.

His likeness followed me in sleep,
Always endearing, always loving:
A thousand times, beloved mother,
You surprised a burning sigh on my lips.
It was he who tore it from my breast;
He, the spellbinder of my senses;
He, the ideal of my most amorous dreams;
He, my first, my fervent love.

Without him, the joyful meadows
Gave me thorns instead of blossoms.
Without him, the sun of the month of April
Filtered shadows into my eyes.
His love was the center of my soul;
I lived in his passionate life.
He my ambition, he my pride...
Why did the villain forget me so quickly?

He loves me no longer, he fancies another.
His caresses are as cold as ice.
His fidelity's a lie, he feigns apprehension...
But he won't deceive me with his falsehoods...
Oh I could love him, delirious, crazy!
No, my pride won't suffer his cruelty!
And heart, if you can't forget the scoundrel,
I shall tear you from my breast!

—*Robert L. Smith and Judith Candullo*

LIEDER

¡Oh mujer! ¿Por qué siendo tan pura vienen a proyectarse sobre los blancos rayos que despide tu frente las impías sombras de los vicios de la Tierra? ¿Por qué los hombres derraman sobre ti la inmundicia de sus excesos, despreciando y aborreciendo después en su moribundo cansancio lo horrible de sus desórdenes y de sus caleturientos delirios?...

Después del primer destello de tu juventud inocente, todo lo que viene a manchar de cieno los blancos ropajes con que te vistieron las primeras alboradas de tu infancia, y a extinguir tus olorosas esencias y borrar las imágenes de la virtud en tu pensamiento, todo te lo transmiten ellos, todo... y, sin embargo, te desprecian...

ÉSTE VAISE I AQUÉL VAISE

Éste vaise i aquél vaise,
e todos, todos se van.
Galicia, sin homes quedas
que te poidan traballar.
Tes, en cambio, orfos e orfas
e campos de soledad,
e nais que non teñen fillos
e fillos que non tén pais.
E tes corazóns que sufren
longas ausencias mortás,
viudas de vivos e mortos
que ninguén consolará.

AGORA CABELOS NEGROS

Agora cabelos negros,
máis tarde cabelos brancos;
agora dentes de prata,

ROSALÍA DE CASTRO
(SPAIN, 1837–1885)

LIEDER

O woman! Why, being so pure, are the clear rays emanating from
your forehead darkened by the impious shadows of worldly vices?
Why do men pour upon you the filth of their excesses, then detest
you when you fall exhausted, made all the more ghastly by their
debaucheries?...

After the first flush of your innocent youth come maturity and
sobriety to spatter with mud the white gowns you wore during
childhood, and blot out the images of virtue in your thought—
everything they transmit to you, everything...and all that
notwithstanding, they despise you...

—*Ángel Flores and Kate Flores*

THIS ONE GOES AND THAT ONE GOES

This one goes and that one goes,
and all of them, all of them go away;
Galicia, you are left without men
able to work your soil.
Instead you have orphaned boys and orphaned girls
and fields of solitude,
and mothers who have no sons
and sons who have no father.
And you have hearts that suffer
long deathly absences,
widows of the living as well as of the dead
who cannot be consoled.

—*Kate Flores*

TODAY BLACK HAIR

Today black hair,
later gray hair;
today gleaming teeth,

mañán chavellos querbados;
hoxe fazulas de rosas,
mañán de coiro enrugado.

Morte negra, morte negra,
cura de dores e engaños:
¿por qué non mátalas mozas
antes que as maten os anos?

¡JUSTICIA DE LOS HOMBRES! YO TE BUSCO

¡Justicia de los hombres!, yo te busco
pero sólo te encuentro
en la "palabra," que tu nombre aplaude
mientras te niega tenazmente el "hecho."

—Y tú, ¿dónde resides?—me pregunto
con aflicción—, justicia de los cielos!
cuando el pecado es obra de un instante,
y durará la expiación terrible.
¡Mientras dure el Infierno!

DEL RUMOR CADENCIOSO DE LA ONDA

Del rumor cadencioso de la onda
   y el viento que muge,
del incierto reflejo que alumbra
   la selva y la nube;
del piar de alguna ave de paso,
del agreste ignorado perfume
   que el céfiro roba
   al valle o a la cumbre,
mundos hay donde encuentran asilo
   las almas que al peso
   del mundo sucumben.

tomorrow broken teeth;
today pink cheeks,
tomorrow wrinkles.

   Black death, black death,
cure for sorrows and betrayals:
Why do you not kill young girls
before the years kill them?

—*Kate Flores*

JUSTICE OF MEN! I LOOK FOR YOU

Justice of men! I look for you
but I find it is only
in the *word* your name is honored
while in the *deed* you are unfailingly denied.

And you, divine justice! Where are you to be found?
I ask myself in affliction,
when sin is the work of an instant,
but endures in terrible expiation
as long as the fires of hell!

—*Kate Flores*

FROM THE CADENCED ROAR OF THE WAVES

From the cadenced roar of the waves
   and the wail of the wind,
from the shimmering light
   flecked over woodland and cloud,
from the cries of passing birds
and the wild unknown perfumes
   stolen by zephyrs
   from mountaintops and valleys,
there are realms where souls
   crushed by the weight of the world
   find refuge.

—*Kate Flores*

SINTIÉNDOSE ACABAR CON EL ESTÍO

Sintiéndose acabar con el estío
la deshauciada enferma,
¡moriré en el otoño!
—pensó, entre melancólica y contenta—,
y sentiré rodar sobre mi tumba
las hojas también muertas.

Mas...ni aun la muerte complacerla quiso,
cruel también con ella;
perdonóle la vida en el invierno,
y, cuando todo renacía en la tierra,
la mató lentamente entre los himnos
alegres de la hermosa primavera.

NACER HOMBRE

¡Cuánto trabajo ella pasa
por corregir la torpeza
de su esposo, y en la casa!
(Permitidme que me asombre.)
Tan inepto como fatuo,
sigue él siendo la cabeza,
¡Porque es hombre!

Si algunos versos escribe,
de alguno esos versos son,
qu ella solo los suscribe.
(Permitidme que me asombre.)
Si ese alguno no es poeta,
¿Por qué tal suposición?
¡Porque es hombre!

Una mujer superior
en elecciones no vota,
y vota el pillo peor.

FEELING HER END WOULD COME WITH SUMMER'S END

Feeling her end would come with summer's end,
the incurable invalid
thought with mingled joy and sadness:
"I shall die in the autumn,
and over my grave I shall feel the rustling
of the leaves that will also be dead."

But...cruel with her too, not even death
would oblige her,
sparing her life through the winter
and, when all the earth was being born anew,
killing her slowly amidst the happy hymns
of glorious spring.

—*Kate Flores*

ADELA ZAMUDIO
(BOLIVIA, 1854–1928)

TO BE BORN MALE

How she labors without end
to correct her husband's boorishness
about the house!
(Pardon my astonishment.)
Inept as he is fatuous,
he remains the big boss,
Because he's a male!

If a woman writes some verses
they're attributed to some man,
even if she has signed them.
(Pardon my astonishment.)
If that man's no kind of poet
why be so presumptuous?
Because he's a male!

A superior woman
doesn't vote in elections,
but the worst scoundrel can vote.

(Permitidme que me asombre.)
Con tal que aprenda a firmar
puede votar un idiota,
¡Porque es hombre!

Él se abate y bebe o juega
en un revés de la suerte:
ella sufre, lucha y ruega.
(Permitidme que me asombre.)
Que a ella se llame el ''ser débil''
y a él se le llame el ''ser fuerte,''
¡Porque es hombre!

Ella debe perdonar
siéndole su esposo infiel;
pero él se puede vengar.
(Permitidme que me asombre.)
En un caso semejante
hasta puede matar él,
¡Porque es hombre!

¡Oh, mortal privilegiado,
que de perfecto y cabal
gozas seguro renombre!
En todo caso, para esto,
te ha bastado
nacer hombre.

EL HOMBRE

Cuando abrasado por la sed del alma
quiere el hombre, viajero del desierto,
laureles recoger,
al dintel de las puertas de la gloria,
''Detente aquí,'' le dice a la mujer.

Y al volver a emprender la ardua carrera,
si siente que flaquea su valor
''Ven, ven,'' le dice entonces,
''tu eres mi compañera
en las horas de lucha y de dolor.''

(Pardon my astonishment.)
If he can learn to sign his name,
an idiot is allowed to vote,
Because he's a male!

If he's blue and drinks or gambles
when Lady Luck abandons him:
she suffers, struggles, prays.
(Pardon my astonishment.)
She's called "the weaker sex"
while he is called "the stronger,"
Because he's a male!

She must always be indulgent
when her husband proves unfaithful;
but he's allowed to take revenge.
(Pardon my astonishment.)
If she dares to turn the tables
he can even murder her,
Because he's a male!

Oh, most privileged of mortals,
who, most perfect and complete,
enjoys unshakable renown!
For this, in any case,
it has been quite enough, simply,
to have been born a male!

—*Robert L. Smith and Judith Candullo*

MANHOOD

When, parched by the thirst of his soul,
man, traveler in the desert,
gathers up his laurels
at the threshold of the doorway to glory,
"Stay here!" he tells his wife.

But when, turning to an arduous undertaking,
he feels his courage flagging,
"Come, come," he tells her then—
"You are my companion
in my time of struggle and pain."

—*Kate Flores*

RAZONES DE UNA POETISA

Vosotros que murmurais
Sin tener quizás razón
Y a la mujer condenais
Tan solo por que dudais
Que tenga imajinación:
　Vosotros que sin conciencia
De vuestra opinión sutil,
Decis que saber y ciencia
Son de hombres de experiencia,
No del sexo femenil.
　Y emitís el parecer
De que la escoba, el puchero,
Primorosa en el cocer
Y no mirar un tintero,
Es misión de la mujer...
　¿Creeis que la flor trasplantada
En su más risueña infancia,
Del valle de la ignorancia
A una selva cultivada,
Adquiere brillo y fragancia?
　Así también la mujer
Que recibe ilustración
Desde la infancia, ha de ser
En la edad de la razón
Más exacta en su deber...
　Cuántas veces lentamente
Con plácida inspiración
Formé una octava en mi mente
¿Y mi aguja dilijente
Remendaba un pantalón!
　Una producción de Heredia
Recitaba entusiasmada
Tomando punto a una media:
Ved, pues, que no impide nada
Al alma que el genio asedia.
　Y si algun día el destino
Me obliga a barrer mi alcoba,

ANONYMOUS
(CUBA, FL. 1878)

REASONINGS OF A WOMAN POET*

You men who hold forth
Without any reason,
Accusing all women,
Merely because you doubt it,
Of lacking imagination:
    You who without awareness
Of the bias of your opinion
Declare learning and knowledge
The domain of men
And not of the female sex,
    And pontificate
That the broom, the cook-pot,
Elegant cuisine
With never a glance at the inkwell
Is the mission of women...
    Do you not think a flower transplanted
In the bloom of its infancy
From the valley of ignorance
To a cultivated garden
Gains luster and fragrance?
    So, too, a woman
Who is given enlightenment
From childhood, must be,
At the age of reason,
More exacting in her duties...
    How many times have I slowly
With quiet inspiration
Shaped in my mind a stanza
While my diligent needle
Was mending a pair of pants!
    Or, rhapsodically reciting
A poem of Heredia,
Have I, transported by his genius,
Been darning a pair of socks!
    And if some day my destiny
Makes me clean up my room,
Will you think it ridiculous

*This poem appeared on February 23, 1878, in *El Áncora*, a Mexico City working-class
weekly that was the organ of Popularmexicana del Trabajo, a labor union.

Creeréis que haga un desatino?
Vereis manejar con tino
A una poetisa, una escoba. .
   Y despúés que concluyera
El deber que me imponía,
¿Qué particular tuviera
Que inspirada yo escribiera
Una dulce poesía?. . .
Estas son las reflexiones
Hombres, que debéis hacer,
No injustas acusaciones,
Ni dar falsas opiniones
En contra de la mujer.

OTRA ESTIRPE

Eros, yo quiero guiarte, Padre ciego ..
pido a tus manos todopoderosas
¡su cuerpo excelso derramado en fuego
sobre mi cuerpo desmayado en rosas!

La eléctrica corola que hoy despliego
brinda el nectario de un jardín de Esposas;
para sus buitres en mi carne entrego
todo un enjambre de palomas rosas.

Da a las dos sierpes de su abrazo, crueles,
mi gran tallo febril... Absintio, mieles,
viérteme de sus venas, de su boca...

¡Así tendida, soy un surco ardiente
donde puede nutrirse la simiente
de otra Estirpe sublimemente loca!

To see the skill
Of a poet holding a broom?
   And if, after I have finished
The task imposed on me,
How odd would it be
If I were to write inspired,
Lovely poetry?...
   This is the reasoning
You ought to have, men,
Not unjust accusations,
Not erroneous opinions
Against women.

—*Robert L. Smith and Judith Candullo*

DELMIRA AGUSTINI
(URUGUAY, 1886–1914)

ANOTHER BREED

Eros, I wish to guide you, blind Father...
give me your almighty hands,
your superb body pouring in fire
across my body pallid in the midst of roses!

The electric corolla I unfold today
toasts with the nectar of a garden of Wives:
an entire swarm of rosy doves in my flesh
I surrender to your vultures.

To the two cruel serpents of your embrace
give my long fevered trunk... Absinthe, honeys,
pour me from their veins, from their mouths...

Thus outstretched I am a burning furrow
where can be nurtured the seed
of another sublimely demented Breed!

—*Kate Flores*

LO INEFABLE

Yo muero extrañamente... No me mata la Vida,
no me mata la Muerte, no me mata el Amor;
muero de un pensamiento mudo como una herida.

¿No habéis sentido nunca el extraño dolor
de un pensamiento inmenso que se arraiga en la vida,
devorando alma y carne, y no alcanza a dar flor?
¿Nunca llevásteis dentro una estrella dormida
que os abrasaba enteros y no daba un fulgor...?

¡Cumbre de los Martirios...! ¡Llevar eternamente
desgarradora y árida, la trágica simiente
clavada en las entrañas como un diente feroz...!

Pero arrancarla un día en una flor que abriera
milagrosa, inviolable... ¡Ah, más grande no fuera
tener entre las manos la cabeza de Dios!

LA EXTRANJERA

—"Habla con dejo de sus mares bárbaros,
con no sé qué algas y no sé qué arenas;
reza oración a dios sin bulto y peso,
envejecida como si muriera.
Ese huerto nuestro que nos hizo extraño,
ha puesto cactus y zarpadas hierbas.
Alienta del resuello del desierto
y ha amado con pasión de que blanquea,
que nunca cuenta y que si nos contase
sería como el mapa de otra estrella.
Vivirá entre nosotros ochenta años,
pero siempre será como si llega,
hablando lengua que jadea y gime
y que le entienden sólo bestezuelas.
Y va a morirse en medio de nosotros,

THE INEFFABLE

I die a strange death... Life does not kill me,
Death does not kill me, Love does not kill me;
I die of a thought silent as a wound.

Have you never felt the strange pain
of an immense thought which takes root in life,
devouring soul and flesh, and without ever reaching fruition?
Have you never carried within you a dormant star
which burned you utterly without shedding any radiance?

Most exquisite martyrdom! To bear eternally,
lacerating and sterile, this tragic seed
nailed to one's entrails like a terrible tooth!

But to extract it one day, in a flower unfolding,
miraculous, inviolable... Ah, there can be nothing greater
than to hold within one's hands the head of God!

—*Kate Flores*

GABRIELA MISTRAL
(CHILE, 1889–1957)

THE ALIEN

"She speaks with the accent of her savage seas,
of I know not what seaweeds, I know not what sands;
she prays to a god without bulk or weight,
aged to the point of dying.
This garden of ours she estranged from us
and sowed it with cactus and thorn.
She exudes the breath of the wilderness,
and she loved with a parching passion
she never tells about, and which, if she did,
would be like the map of another star.
She will live among us for eighty years,
but always seem newly arrived,
uttering a language that gasps and moans
and only beasts of the field understand.
And she is going to die in our midst

en una noche en la que más padezca,
con sólo su destino por almohada,
de una muerte callada y *extranjera.*"

EMIGRADA JUDÍA

Voy más lejos que el viento oeste
y el petrel de tempestad.
Paro, interrogo, camino
¡y no duermo por caminar!
Me rebanaron la Tierra,
sólo me han dejado el mar.

Se quedaron en la aldea
casa, costumbre, y dios lar.
Pasan tilos, carrizales
y el Rin que me enseñó a hablar.
No llevo al pecho las mentas
cuyo olor me haga llorar.
Tan sólo llevo mi aliento
y mi sangre y mi ansiedad.

Una soy a mis espaldas,
otra volteada al mar:
mi nuca hierve de adioses,
y mi pecho de ansiedad.

Ya el torrente de mi aldea
no da mi nombre al rodar
y en mi tierra y aire me borro
como huella en arenal.

A cada trecho de ruta
voy perdiendo mi caudal:
una oleada de resinas,
una torre, un robledal.
Suelta mi mano sus gestos
de hacer la sidra y el pan
y aventada mi memoria
llegaré desnuda al mar!

some night of her worst affliction
with only her fate for a pillow
of a death unspoken and *alien*.''

—*Kate Flores*

ÉMIGRÉ JEWESS

Farther than the west wind I am going,
farther than the stormy petrel.
I stop, I ask, I walk,
and do not sleep in order to walk!
They sliced the Land from under me,
I am left with only the sea.

Left behind in my village
house, customs, and tutelary god.
Past linden trees, reed-fields
and the Rhine which taught me to speak.
I do not press to my breast the mint
whose fragrance would make me weep.
I carry only my breath
and my blood and my anguish.

My back is one person,
another is turned toward the sea:
my nape seething with farewells,
and my breast with anguish.

The river of my village no longer
speaks my name as it flows,
and in my land and air I am effaced
like a footprint in the sand.

With every stretch of the way
I go on losing my fortune:
a whiff of resins,
a tower, a grove of oaks.
My hands let go the gestures
of making cider and bread,
and stripped of my remembrance
I shall naked reach the sea!

—*Kate Flores*

HOMBRE PEQUEÑITO

Hombre pequeñito, hombre pequeñito,
Suelta a tu canario que quiere volar...
Yo soy el canario, hombre pequeñito,
Déjame saltar.

Estuve en tu jaula, hombre pequeñito,
Hombre pequeñito que jaula me das.
Digo pequeñito porque no me entiendes,
Ni me entenderás.

Tampoco te entiendo, pero mientras tanto
Ábreme la jaula que quiero escapar;
Hombre pequeñito, te amé media hora,
No me pidas más.

OLVIDO

Lidia Rosa: hoy es martes y hace frío. En tu casa,
De piedra gris, tú duermes tu sueño en un costado
De la ciudad. ¿Aún guardas tu pecho enamorado,
Ya que de amor moriste? Te diré lo que pasa:

El hombre que adorabas, de grises ojos crueles,
En la tarde de otoño fuma su cigarrillo.
Detrás de los cristales mira el cielo amarillo
Y la calle en que vuelan desteñidos papeles.

Toma un libro, se acerca a la apagada estufa,
En el tomacorriente al sentarse la enchufa
Y sólo se oye un ruido de papel desgarrado.

Las cinco. Tú caías a esta hora en su pecho,
Y acaso te recuerda... Pero su blanco lecho
Ya tiene el hueco tibio de otro cuerpo rosado.

ALFONSINA STORNI
(ARGENTINA, 1892–1938)

SMALL MAN

Small man, small man,
Let free your canary that wants to fly...
I am the canary, small man,
Let me go.

I have been in your cage, small man,
Small man who gives me a cage.
I say you are small because you do not understand me,
And will never understand me.

Nor will I you; but for now
Open the cage, for I wish to escape;
Small man, I loved you for half an hour,
Ask of me no more.

—*Kate Flores*

FORGETTING

Lídia Rosa: today is Tuesday and it is cold. In your house
Of grey stone you sleep your sleep on the outskirts
Of the town. Do you still have love in your breast,
You who died of love? Let me tell you what is happening:

The man whom you adored, of cruel grey eyes,
Is smoking his cigarette this autumn afternoon.
From his window he looks out at the yellow sky
And the street where faded papers blow about.

He takes a book, comes near the extinguished stove,
And as he sits down he plugs in the socket,
And only a sound of crumpled paper can be heard.

Five o'clock. You used to lie on his breast at this hour,
And perhaps he remembers you... But already your white bed
Holds the warm hollow of another rosy body.

—*Kate Flores*

TU ME QUIERES BLANCA

Tú me quieres alba;
me quieres de espumas;
me quieres de nácar.
Que sea azucena,
sobre todas, casta.
De perfume tenue.
Corola cerrada.

Ni un rayo de luna
filtrado me haya
ni una margarita
se diga mi hermana;
tú me quieres blanca;
tú me quieres nívea;
tú me quieres casta.

Tú, que hubiste todas
las copas a mano,
de frutos y mieles
los labios morados.
Tú, que en el banquete,
cubierto de pámpanos,
dejaste las carnes
festejando a Baco.
Tú, que en los jardines
negros del engaño,
vestido de rojo,
corriste al Estrago.

Tú, que el esqueleto
conservas intacto,
no sé todavía
por cuáles milagros
(Dios te lo perdone),
me pretendes casta
(Dios te lo perdone),
me pretendes alba.
Huye hacia los bosques;
vete a la montaña;
límpiate la boca;
vive en las cabañas;
toca con las manos
la tierra mojada;
alimenta el cuerpo

YOU WOULD HAVE ME IMMACULATE

You would have me immaculate,
you would have me seaspray,
you would have me pearl,
that I be of lilies
the chastest of all,
my perfume subdued,
corolla enclosed.

Not a ray of moonlight
must filter to me,
nor may a daisy
be said to be my sister;
unsullied you would have me;
you would have me snow;
you would have me chaste.

You whose hands
have held all the goblets,
whose lips are purple
with honey and fruits,
you who at banquets
covered with vine leaves
passed over the meat
to feast with Bacchus,
you who in gardens
dark with deceit,
clad in scarlet,
caroused to ruin.

You whose skeleton
you keep intact
by what miracles
I still do not know
(may God forgive you),
expect me to be chaste
(may God forgive you),
expect me to be pure.
Be off to the woods;
get away to the mountain;
clean out your mouth;
live in a shack;
touch with your hands
the humid earth;
feed your body

con raíz amarga;
bebe de las rocas;
duerme sobre escarcha;
renueva tejidos
con salitre y agua;
habla con los pájaros
y lávate al alba.
Y cuando las carnes
te sean tornadas,
y cuando hayas puesto
en ellas el alma,
que por las alcobas
se quedó enredada,
entonces, buen hombre,
preténdeme blanca,
preténdeme nívea,
preténdeme casta.

LA QUE COMPRENDE

Con la cabeza negra caída hacia adelante
Está la mujer bella, la de mediana edad,
Postrada de rodillas, y un Cristo agonizante
Desde su duro leño la mira con piedad.

En los ojos la carga de una enorme tristeza,
En el seno la carga del hijo por nacer,
Al pie del blanco Cristo que está sangrando reza:
—¡Señor, el hijo mío que no nazca mujer!

with bitter roots;
drink from the rocks;
sleep on the frost;
restore your tissue
with saltpeter and water;
converse with the birds
and arise with the dawn.
And when your flesh
has returned to your bones,
and you have given it back
the soul you left
entangled in bedrooms,
then, good man,
expect me to be immaculate,
expect me to be snow-white,
expect me to be chaste.

—*Kate Flores*

SHE WHO UNDERSTANDS

With her black hair fallen forward,
The beautiful woman, of middle age,
Is prostrate on her knees, while a Christ in agony
From his wooden cross looks down upon her with pity.

In her eyes the burden of an enormous sadness,
In her breast the burden of a child to be born,
At the foot of the pale bleeding Christ she prays:
"Lord, let not my child be born woman!"

—*Kate Flores*

PESO ANCESTRAL

Tú me dijiste: no lloró mi padre;
tú me dijiste: no lloró mi abuelo;
no han llorado los hombres de mi raza,
eran de acero.

Así diciendo te brotó una lágrima
y me cayó en la boca...más veneno.
Yo no he bebido nunca en otro vaso
así pequeño.

Débil mujer, pobre mujer que entiende,
dolor de siglos conocí al beberlo:
Oh, el alma mía soportar no puede
todo su peso.

PALABRAS A DELMIRA AGUSTINI

Estás muerta y tu cuerpo, bajo uruguayo manto
Descansa de su fuego, se limpia de su llama,
Sólo desde tus libros tu roja lengua llama
Como cuando vivías, al amor y al encanto.

Hoy, si un alma de tantas, sentenciosa y oscura,
Con palabras pesadas va a sangrarte el oído,
Encogida en tu pobre cajoncito roído
No puedes contestarle desde tu sepultura.

Pero sobre tu pecho, para siempre deshecho,
Comprensivo vigila, todavía, mi pecho,
Y, si ofendida lloras por tus cuencas abiertas

Tus lágrimas heladas, con mano tan liviana
Que más que mano amiga parece mano hermana,
Te enjugo dulcemente las tristes cuencas muertas.

ANCESTRAL WEIGHT

You told me my father never wept;
nor did my grandfather weep;
the men of my line never wept;
they were of steel.

And as you were speaking, a tear
slipped from your eye, and fell into my mouth...
Never have I drunk such poison
from a cup so small.

Weak woman, wretched woman who comprehends
the sorrow of the centuries I knew when I drank:
Oh, my soul is not able to bear
all that weight!

—*Kate Flores*

WORDS FOR DELMIRA AGUSTINI

You are dead and your body, beneath a Uruguayan cloak,
Rests from its fires, casts aside its flame;
Only from your books does your red tongue call
As when you were alive, to love and enchantment.

Today, if some soul among so many, sententious and obscure,
With weighty words comes to bleed your ear,
Shrunk in your poor worn little coffin,
You cannot answer him from your grave.

But over your breast, forever destroyed,
Still my breast, understanding, keeps watch;
And if, offended, through your empty hollows you weep

Your frozen tears, with a hand so tender
It will seem not a friend's hand but that of a sister,
I shall dry sweetly your sad dead hollows.

—*Kate Flores*

PUDIERA SER

Pudiera ser que todo lo que en verso he sentido
no fuera más que aquello que nunca pudo ser,
no fuera más que algo vedado y reprimido
de familia en familia, de mujer en mujer.

Dicen que en los solares de mi gente medido
estaba todo aquello que se debía hacer...
Dicen que silenciosas las mujeres han sido
de mi casa materna... ¡Ah!, bien pudiera ser...

A veces en mi madre apuntaron antojos
de liberarse, pero se le subió a los ojos
una honda amargura, y en la sombra lloró.

Y todo esto mordiente, vendido, mutilado,
todo esto que se hallaba en su alma encerrado
pienso que, sin quererlo, lo he libertado yo.

DOLOR

Quisiera esta tarde divina de octubre
pasear por la orilla lejana del mar;

que la arena de oro y las aguas verdes
y los cielos puros me vieran pasar.

Ser alta, soberbia, perfecta, quisiera,
como una romana, para concordar

con las grandes olas, y las rocas muertas
y las anchas playas que ciñen el mar.

Con el paso lento y los ojos fríos
y la boca muda dejarme llevar;

ver cómo se rompen las olas azules
contra los granitos, y no parpadear;

ver cómo las aves rapaces se comen
los peces pequeños, y no suspirar;

pensar que pudieran las frágiles barcas
hundirse en las aguas, y no despertar;

IT COULD BE

It could be that all that imbues my verse
is simply what never came to be,
simply what was suppressed and left unspoken,
family after family, woman after woman.

They say that on the estates of my father
the rule was absolute propriety...
They say that in the home of my mother
the women were silent... Ah! it well could be...

There were times when my mother had longings
for freedom, but a bitter wave
would well up in her eyes, and in the dark she would weep.

And all that abuse, abasement, contempt,
all that she kept locked up in her soul,
I think I may have somehow, unconsciously, set free.

—*Kate Flores*

ACHING

I should like on this divine October afternoon
to stroll along a distant shore of the sea,

where the golden sand and the green waters
and the pure skies could watch me go by.

Tall, haughty, superb, I should like to be,
like a Roman woman, to harmonize

with the great waves and the dead rocks
and the wide beaches that gird the sea.

With slow step and cold eye
and muted voice, to let myself go;

to see how the blue waves crash
against the granite, without blinking;

to see how the rapacious birds devour
the little fishes, without sighing;

to think that the frail boats can sink
beneath the waters, without waking;

ver que se adelanta, la garganta libre,
el hombre más bello; no desear amar...

Perder la mirada, distraídamente,
perderla, y que nunca la vuelva a encontrar;

y, figura erguida, entre cielo y playa,
sentirme el olvido perenne del mar.

VOY A DORMIR

Dientes de flores, cofia de rocío,
manos de hierbas, tú, nodriza fina,
tenme prestas la sábanas terrosas
y el edredón de musgos escardados.

Voy a dormir, nodriza mía, acuéstame.
Ponme una lámpara a la cabecera;
una constelación; la que te guste;
todas son buenas; bájala un poquito.

Déjame sola: oyes romper los brotes...
te acuna un pie celeste desde arriba
y un pájaro te traza unos compases

para que olvides... Gracias. Ah, un encargo:
si él llama nuevamente por teléfono
le dices que no insista, que he salido...

to see approaching, his throat free,
the most beautiful man, without wanting to love...

To lose my gaze, uncaringly,
to lose it never to find it again;

and, figure upright, between sky and shore,
to feel within me the endless forgetfulness of the sea.

—*Kate Flores*

I AM GOING TO SLEEP*

With teeth of flowers, headdress of dew,
hands of grass, prepare for me
my earthen sheets, good wetnurse,
and my quilt of weedy moss.

I am going to sleep, my wetnurse, put me to bed.
Put a lamp at my headboard for me:
a constellation; any one you like;
all are good; lower it a bit.

Leave me alone: you can hear the buds breaking...
a heavenly foot rocks your cradle from above,
and a bird is tracing out melodies for you

so that you can forget... Thank you. Ah, one favor:
if he telephones again
tell him not to keep trying, that I have gone away...

—*Kate Flores*

*This poem appeared in the Buenos Aires newspaper
La Nación the morning after Storni's suicide.

REBELDE

Caronte: yo seré un escándalo en tu barca.
Mientras las otras sombras recen, giman, o lloren,
y bajo tus miradas de siniestro patriarca
las tímidas y tristes, en bajo acento, oren,

yo iré como una alondra cantando por el río
y llevaré a tu barca mi perfume salvaje,
e irradiaré en las ondas del arroyo sombrío
como una azul linterna que alumbrara en el viaje.

Por más que tú no quieras, por más guiños siniestros
que me hagan tus dos ojos, en el terror maestros,
Caronte, yo en tu barca seré como un escándalo.

Y extenuada de sombra, de valor y de frío,
cuando quieras dejarme a la orilla del río
me bajarán tus brazos cual conquista de vándalo.

¡MUJER!

Si yo fuera hombre, ¡qué hartazgo de luna,
de sombra y silencio me había de dar!
¡Cómo, noche a noche, solo ambularía
por los campos quietos y por frente al mar!

Si yo fuera hombre, ¡que extraño, que loco,
tenaz vagabundo que había de ser!
Amigo de todos los largos caminos
que invitan a ir lejos para no volver!

Cuando así me acosan ansias andariegas
¡qué pena tan honda me da ser mujer!

JUANA DE IBARBOUROU
(ARGENTINA, 1895–1979)

REBEL

Charon:* I shall be a scandal on your ferry.
While the other shades pray, moan or weep,
and under the eyes of the sinister patriarch,
timid and sad, worship in whispers,

I shall go like a lark, singing down the river
and bring to your ship my wild perfume,
I shall light up the waves of the somber stream,
like a blue lantern I shall brighten the journey.

Despite the sinister glances from both your eyes,
two masters of terror, against all your wishes,
Charon, in your boat I shall be a scandal.

And when, weary with the dark, the strain and the cold,
you wish to drop me off by the side of the river,
your arms will lower me as if in conquest of a vandal.

—*Kate Flores*

WOMAN!

   If I were a man, in what a wealth of moon,
of shade and of silence I should revel!
How, night after night, I should merely wander
through quiet fields and along the shores of the sea!

   If I were a man, what a strange, what a mad,
inveterate vagabond I should be!
Friend of all the meandering roadways
that beckon one to go far away, never to return!

   When thus besieged by the need to roam
how painful it is to be a woman!

—*Kate Flores*

*In Greek mythology Charon is the boatman who
ferried dead souls across the river Styx to Hades.

de DIOS, NUESTRA SEÑORA

Mujer, Madre del Hombre.
Humillada hasta lo más profundo de tu ser.
Para el fraile eres la imagen del pecado;
para el político, instrumento de placer;
para el artista, quizás un tema estético
y para el sabio,
un "caso" que no ha podido resolver...
Y eres nada, eres nadie, en el momento
en que juegan la vida de tus hijos.
Te utilizan en "planes pacifistas"
y disparan la muerte masiva a tus espaldas.
Para tí, la traición y la ignominia
en la más insolente desventaja.
La milenaria esclavitud que sufres
te apartó del sendero de la sabiduría
dando la vida a quien la vida no ama.
Tú, mujer solitaria, también te has extraviado.
¡Oh, Madre indestructible
que posees la clave de la vida!
¡Ya levántate y habla!

CONCHA MICHEL
(MEXICO, 1899–)

from GOD, OUR LADY

Woman, Mother of Man.
Humiliated to the depths of your being.
For the friar you are the image of sin;
for the politician, instrument of pleasure;
for the artist, an aesthetic theme, perhaps,
and for the scholar
a "case" he cannot solve...
And you have been nothing, you have been nobody,
as they toyed with the lives of your sons.
They use you for "pacifist plans"
and shoot to kill behind your back.
For you ignominy and treachery
in the utmost degradation.
    The millennial enslavement you have suffered
has kept you from the path of learning,
giving life to those not loved by life.
Lonely woman, you too have lost your way.
O, indestructible Mother
who holds the key to life!
Rise up at last and speak!

—*Kate Flores*

MUJERES DEL MERCADO

Son de cal y salmuera. Viejas ya desde siempre.
Armadura oxidada con relleno de escombros.
Tienen duros los ojos como fría cellisca.
Los cabellos marchitos como hierba pisada
y un vinagre maligno les recorre las venas.

Van temprano a la compra. Huronean los puestos.
Casi escarban. Eligen los tomates chafados.
Las naranjas mohosas. Maceradas verduras
que ya huelen a estiércol. Compran sangre cocida
en cilindros oscuros como quesos de lodo
y esos bofes que muestran, sonrosados y túmidos,
una obscena apariencia.

Al pagar, un suspiro les separa los labios
explorando morosas en el vientre mugriento
de un enorme y raído monedero sin asas
con un miedo feroz a topar de improviso
en su fondo la última cochambrosa moneda.

Siempre llevan un niño todo greñas y mocos
que les cuelga y arrastra de la falda pringosa
chupeteando una monda de manzana o de plátano.
Lo manejan a gritos, a empellones. Se alejan
maltratando el esparto de la sucia alpargata.

Van a un patio con moscas. Con chiquillos y perros.
Con vecinas que riñen. A un fogón pestilente.
A un barreño de ropa por lavar. A un marido
con olor a aguardiente, a sudor y a colilla.
Que mastica en silencio. Que blasfema y escupe.
Que tal vez por la noche en la fétida alcoba,
sin caricias ni halagos, con brutal impaciencia
de animal instintivo, les castigue la entraña
con el peso agobiante de otro mísero fruto.
Otro largo cansancio.

¡Oh, no! Yo no pretendo pedir explicaciones.
Pero hay cielos tan puros. Existe la belleza.

ANGELA FIGUERA-AYMERICH
(SPAIN, 1902–1984)

MARKET WOMEN

They're of lime and brine. Old since the beginning of time.
Rusted shells filled with rubbish.
Their eyes are hard like cold sleet.
Hair withered like trampled turf,
and through their veins a malignant vinegar flows.

They go shopping early. They poke around the stands.
They practically dig. They choose the crushed tomatoes.
The rotting oranges. The mauled vegetables
that smell already like manure. They buy cooked blood,
dark like cylindrical cheeses of mud,
and those lungs that seem, blushing and timid,
to be obscene.

When they pay, a sigh separates their lips
as they rummage reluctantly through the filthy belly
of a huge tattered handbag without handles,
fearing by some chance unexpectedly to find
in its depths their last stinking piece of money.

Always they have with them a child, sniveling and disheveled,
clinging and pulling their greasy skirt,
sucking an apple or banana peel.
They control them with shoves, with shouts. Punishing
the rope soles of their dirty sandals, they go away.

They go to a courtyard full of flies. Of kids and dogs.
Of neighbor women quarreling. To a pestilential cookstove.
To a tub of clothes to be washed. To a husband
smelly with liquor, sweat and cigarette butts.
Who chews in silence. Who curses and spits.
Who perhaps at night, in the fetid alcove,
without caress or tenderness, with the brute impatience
of animal instinct, oppresses their entrails
with the burden of another miserable fruit.
Another long weariness.

Oh, no! I do not presume to ask for explanations.
But there are skies so pure. There exists beauty.

—*Kate Flores*

MADRES

Madres del Hombre, úteros fecundos,
hornos de Dios donde se cristaliza
el humus vivo en ordenados moldes.

Para vosotras, madres, no fue sólo
amor un ramalazo por los nervios,
un éxtasis fugaz, una delicia
derretida en olvido.
No fue tan sólo un cuerpo contra otro,
un labio contra otro, una frenética
soldadura de sangres.

Madres del Hombre, dulces, descuidadas
del ojo circular de la serpiente
que irónico se abrió sobre la curva
suave y rosada de Eva sin vestido
con el sapiente fruto entre las manos...

Sólo un tesón humilde, una gozosa
dedicación os rige las entrañas
en esos largos días de la espera.

Gloria y dolor en el instante último
con una tibia flor recién abierta,
tan íntima, tan próxima, latiendo
junto a la propia fatigada carne.
Y luego, ¿qué? Cumplisteis la tarea.
El hijo terminado se levanta
en fuerza y hermosura sobre el suelo.
Desde las piernas de trenzados músculos;
a esa palmera débil que desfleca
el viento sombreándole las sienes,
todo es hechura vuestra, logro vuestro.

Y luego, ¿qué? ¿Qué veis por los caminos
de la tierra en tormenta?
¿Adónde irán los pies qué golpearon
la cárcel sin hendir de vuestro vientre?
¿Qué histéricas ciudades, que paredes
de leproso cemento
lo encerrarán? ¿Qué campos abonados
con aceros y pólvoras
verán crecer la espiga suficiente
al hambre de su boca sin pecado?
¿Qué obsceno sol hará su mediodía?

MOTHERS

Mothers of men, prolific wombs,
God's ovens, where the living humus
is crystallized into shapely forms.

For you, mothers, love was not merely
a sudden shock of nerves,
a fleeting ecstasy, a delight
melting away into oblivion.
It was not merely one body upon another,
one lip upon another, a frenetic
welding of bloods.

Mothers of men, sweet, forgetful
of the circular eye of the serpent
which opened ironically upon the soft
and pink curves of naked Eve,
with the wise fruit between her hands...

Only humble determination, a joyous
dedication governed your innards
during those long days of waiting.

Glory and pain at the final moment,
with a warm blossom newly opened
so intimate, so close, throbbing
beside your own weary flesh.
And then what? You have fulfilled your task.
The finished child lifts himself up
in strength and beauty upon the floor.
From his legs of braided muscles
to the fragile palm tree shading his temples
shaken out by the wind,
everything is of your own making, your own accomplishment.

And then what? What do you see along the road
of this anguished land?
Where will those feet go that kicked
its prison without splitting open your stomach?
What hysterical cities, what walls
of leprous cement
will lock him up? What fields fertilized
with steel and gunpowder
will yield enough
to quench the hunger of his mouth without sin?
What obscene sun will provide his noon?

¿Qué luna sin jazmín y sin ensueño
será gracia y belleza de sus noches?
¿Qué ancho glaciar de fórmulas sin música
lo apresará en su bárbara corriente?
¿Qué implacable mecánica
triturará sus nervios?
¿Qué monstruosa química, qué fiebre
le robarán el rojo de la sangre?
¿Qué plomo, qué aspereza de herramienta
le romperá los músculos?
¿Qué mísera moneda
mancillará sus manos?
¿Qué rabias, qué codicias, qué rencores
harán brotar espinas de sus ojos?
¿Qué muerte apresurada, sin dulzura,
lo pudrirá voraz, en cualquier parte?

Madres del mundo, tristes paridoras,
gemid, clamad, aullad por vuestros frutos.

DESTINO

Vaso me hiciste, hermético alfarero,
y diste a mi oquedad las dimensiones
que sirven a la alquimia de la carne.
Vaso me hiciste, recipiente vivo
para la forma un día diseñada
por el secreto ritmo de tus manos.

Hágase en mí, repuse. Y te bendije
con labios obedientes al destino.

¿Por qué, después me robas y defraudas?

Libre el varón camina por los días.
Sus recias piernas nunca soportaron
esa tremenda gravidez del fruto.
Liso y escueto entre ágiles caderas
su vientre no conoce pesadumbre.
Sólo un instante, furia y goce, olvida
por mí su altiva soledad de macho.

What moon without jasmine and without dreams
will be the grace and beauty of his nights?
What great glacier of formulae without music
will sweep him up in its barbarous current?
What implacable machine
will crush his nerves?
What monstrous alchemy, what fever
will rob him of the redness of his blood?
What lead, what demonical device
will rip his muscles apart?
What dirty coin
will foul his hands?
Out of what rage, what greed, what rancor
will thorns sprout from his eyes?
What sudden death, without sweetness,
will somewhere putrify him?

Mothers of the world, sad procreators,
moan, screech, howl for your fruits.

—*Kate Flores*

DESTINY

You made me a cup, inscrutable potter,
giving to my concavity the dimensions
essential to the alchemy of the flesh.
You made me a cup, living recipient
of the form designed one day
by the secret rhythm of your hands.

Let this be done to me, I replied. And I blessed you
with lips obeisant to destiny.

Why then do you rob me and defraud me?

Unhindered the male strides through his days.
His powerful legs have never to bear
the tremendous weight of the fruit.
Flat and free between his agile hips
his belly experiences no burden.
Only for an instant, in fury and pleasure, does he forget
through me the haughty aloneness of the male.

Libérase a sí mismo y me encadena
al áspero servicio de la especie.
Cuán hondamente exprimo, laborando
con células y fibras, con mis órganos
más íntimos, vitales dulcedumbres
de mi profundo ser, día tras día.

Hácese el hijo en mí. ¿Y han de llamarle
hijo del Hombre cuando, fieramente,
con decisiva urgencia me desgarra
para moverse vivo entre las cosas?
Mío es el hijo en mí y en él me aumento.
Su corazón prosigue mi latido.
Saben a mí sus lágrimas primeras.
Y esa humedad caliente que lo envuelve
es la temperatura de mi entraña.

¿Por qué, Señor, me lo arrebatas luego?
¿Por qué me crece ajeno, desprendido
como amputado miembro, como rama
desconectada del nutricio tronco?

En vano mi ternura lo persigue
queriéndolo ablandar, disminuyéndolo.
Alto se yergue. Duro se condensa.
Su frente sobrepasa mi estatura
y ese pulido azul de sus pupilas
que en rincón de mí cuajó su brillo
me mira desde lejos, olvidando.

Apenas si las yemas de mis dedos
aciertan a seguir por sus mejillas
aquella suave curva que, al beberme,
formaba con la curva de mis senos
dulcísima tangencia.

He liberates himself only to shackle me
in bitter servitude to the species.
From what depths do I give forth, laboring
with every cell and fiber, with my most intimate organs,
the vital sweetness
of my inmost being, one day after another.

The son is made within me. And will they yet call him
the son of Man, when ferociously,
with implacable urgency, he tears me apart
to move about alive amid the things of the world?
Mine is the son within me and with him I am enlarged.
His heart follows my heartbeat.
His first tears taste of me.
And that warm humidity suffusing him
is the temperature of my entrails.

Why then, Lord, do you take him from me?
Why does he grow up another's, separated
as an amputated limb, as a bough
detached from its nurturing trunk?

In vain my tenderness pursues him,
seeking to assuage him, to diminish him.
He straightens up. He hardens.
His forehead rises high above mine,
and that burnished blue of his pupils
which from some corner of me gathered its radiance
looks at me from afar, forgetting.

Scarcely can the tips of my fingers
follow along his cheeks
that soft curve which, when he drank of me,
in sweetest closeness,
followed along the curve of my breasts.

—Kate Flores

A JULIA DE BURGOS

Ya las gentes murmuran que yo soy tu enemiga
porque dicen que en verso doy al mundo tu yo.
Mienten, Julia de Burgos. Mienten, Julia de Burgos.
La que se alza en mis versos no es tu voz: es mi voz;
porque tú eres el ropaje y la esencia soy yo;
y el más profundo abismo se tiende entre las dos.

Tú eres fría muñeca de mentira social,
y yo, viril destello de la humana verdad.

Tú, miel de cortesanas hipocresías; yo no;
que en todos mis poemas desnudo el corazón.

Tú eres como tu mundo, egoísta; yo no;
que todo me lo juego a ser lo que soy yo.

Tú eres sólo la grave señora señorona;
yo no; yo soy la vida, la fuerza, la mujer.

Tú eres de tu marido, de tu amo; yo no;
yo de nadie, o de todos, porque a todos, a todos,
en mi limpio sentir y en mi pensar me doy.

Tú te rizas el pelo y te pintas; yo no;
a mí me riza el viento; a mí me pinta el sol.

Tú eres dama casera, resignada, sumisa,
atada a los prejuicios de los hombres; yo no;
que yo soy Rocinante corriendo desbocado
olfateando horizontes de justicia de Dios.

Tú en ti misma no mandas; a ti todos te mandan;
en ti mandan tu esposo, tus padres, tus parientes,
el cura, la modista, el teatro, el casino,
el auto, las alhajas, el banquete, el champán,
el cielo y el infierno y el qué dirán social.

En mí no, que en mí manda mi solo corazón,
mi solo pensamiento; quien manda en mí soy yo.

Tú flor de aristocracia; y yo la flor del pueblo.
tú en ti lo tienes todo y a todos se lo debes,
mientras que yo, mi nada a nadie se la debo.

JULIA DE BURGOS
(PUERTO RICO, 1914–1958)

TO JULIA DE BURGOS

They say I am your enemy
because I give your inmost self to the world in verse.
They lie, Julia de Burgos. They lie, Julia de Burgos.
The voice that sounds in my poems is not your voice: it is my voice;
because you are the trappings and I am the essence;
and between us stretches the deepest divide.

You are the cold doll of social prevarication,
and I the living spark of human truth.

You are the honey of polite hypocrisies; not I,
who lay bare my naked heart in all my poems.

You are like your world, selfish; not I,
who risk everything to be what I am.

You are only the prim ladylike lady;
not I; I am life, strength, woman.

You belong to your husband, to your master; not I;
I belong to no one, or to everyone, because to everyone, everyone,
I give myself in my pure feeling and my thought.

You curl your hair and paint your face; not I;
My hair is curled by the wind, my face is painted by the sun.

You are a housewife, resigned, submissive,
ruled by the prejudices of men; not I;
I am a runaway Rocinante
sniffing at horizons for the justice of God.

You do not command yourself; everyone commands you:
your husband, your parents, your relatives,
the priest, the dressmaker, the theatre, the casino,
the car, the jewels, the banquet, the champagne,
heaven and hell and social gossip.

Not me; to me only my heart gives commands,
only my thought; the one who commands me is myself.

You, flower of the aristocracy, and I, flower of the people.
You have everything and you owe everything to everyone,
while I, my nothingness I owe to no one.

Tú clavada al estático dividendo ancestral,
y yo, un uno en la cifra del divisor social,
somos el duelo a muerte que se acerca fatal.

Cuando las multitudes corran alborotadas
dejando atrás cenizas de injusticias quemadas,
y cuando con la tea de las siete virtudes,
tras los siete pecados, corran las multitudes,
contra ti y contra todo lo injusto y lo inhumano,
yo iré en medio de ellas con la tea en la mano.

NO SÉ

No sé de dónde soy.
No he nacido en ningún sitio;
yo ya estaba
cuando lo de la manzana,
por eso soy apolítica.
Menos mal que soy mujer,
y no pariré vencejos
ni se mancharán mis manos
con el olor del fusil,
menos mal que soy así. . .

You, nailed to the static ancestral dividend,
and I, a one in the cipher of the social divider,
we are in a duel to the death approaching the inevitable.

While the multitudes race about frantically,
leaving behind ashes from burnt-out injustices,
and while with the torch of the seven virtues
the multitudes pursue the seven sins,
against you, and against everything unjust and inhuman,
I shall go into their midst with the torch in my hand.

—*William M. Davis*

GLORIA FUERTES
(SPAIN, 1918–)

I DON'T KNOW

I don't know where I'm from.
I wasn't born anywhere;
I was here already
before that business about the apple
that's why I'm apolitical.
None the worse that I'm a woman,
and will not give birth to martinets
nor will my hands be soiled
with the smell of guns,
so much the better that I'm this way...

—*Kate Flores*

NO DEJAN ESCRIBIR

Trabajo en un periódico
pude ser secretaria del jefe
y soy sólo mujer de la limpieza.
Sé escribir, pero en mi pueblo,
no dejan escribir a las mujeres.
Mi vida es sin sustancia,
no hago nada malo.
Vivo pobre.
Duermo en casa.
Viajo en Metro.
Ceno un caldo
y un huevo frito, para que luego digan.
Compro libros de viejo,
me meto en las tabernas,
también en los tranvías,
me cuelo en los teatros
y en los saldo me visto.
Hago una vida extraña.

¡HAGO VERSOS, SEÑORES!

Hago versos señores, hago versos,
pero no me gusta que me llamen poetisa,
me gusta el vino como a los albañiles
y tengo una asistenta que habla sola.
Este mundo resulta divertido,
pasan cosas señores que no expongo,
se dan casos, aunque nunca se dan casas
a los pobres que no pueden dar traspaso.
Sigue habiendo solteras con su perro,
sigue habiendo casados con querida,
a los déspotas duros nadie les dice nada,
y leemos que hay muertos y pasamos la hoja,
y nos pisan el cuello y nadie se levanta,
y nos odia la gente y decimos: ¡la vida!
Esto pasa señores y yo debo decirlo.

NOT ALLOWED TO WRITE

I work for a newspaper;
I could be the manager's secretary
and I'm only the cleaning woman.
I know how to write, but in my town
women are not allowed to write.
My life is nothingness.
I don't do anything naughty.
I live poor.
I sleep at home.
I ride the subway.
For supper, broth
and a fried egg, so let them talk.
I buy second-hand books,
I slip into saloons,
also into streetcars,
I sneak into theatres
and dress on bargain sales.
I lead a strange life.

—*Robert L. Smith and Judith Candullo*

I MAKE POEMS, GENTLEMEN!

I make poems gentlemen, I make poems,
but I do not like to be called poetess.
I like wine the same as bricklayers do
and I have an assistant who talks to herself.
This world turns out funny,
things take place gentlemen I cannot explain,
they make cases though never houses,
for the poor who can't give back what for.
Spinsters go walking their dogs,
married men go walking their girlfriends,
to the tough tyrants nobody says a word,
and we read that there are dead and turn the page,
and they step on our necks and no one gets up,
and people despise us and we say: "Such is life!"
This happens, gentlemen, and I have to say it.

—*Kate Flores*

TENER UN HIJO HOY...

Tener un hijo hoy...
para echarle a las manos de los hombres
—si fuera para echarle a las manos de Dios—.
Tener un hijo hoy,
para echarle en la boca del cañón,
abandonarle en la puerta del Dolor,
tirarle al agua de la confusión.
Tener un hijo hoy,
para que pase hambre y sol,
para que no escuche mi voz,
para que luego aprenda la instrucción.
Tener un hijo hoy,
para que le hagan ciego de pasión
o víctima de persecución,
para testigo de la destrucción.
Tener un hijo hoy...
Con él dentro voy,
donde ni él mismo se puede herir,
dónde sólo Dios le hará morir.

LOS PÁJAROS ANIDAN EN MIS BRAZOS

Los pájaros anidan en mis brazos,
en mis hombros, detrás de mis rodillas,
entre los senos tengo codornices,
los pájaros se creen que soy un árbol.
Una fuente se creen que soy los cisnes,
bajan y beben todos cuando hablo.
Las ovejas me pisan cuando pasan,
y comen en mis dedos los gorriones;
se creen que yo soy tierra las hormigas
y los hombres se creen que no soy nada.

TO HAVE A CHILD THESE DAYS...

To have a child these days...
only to deliver him into the hands of men
—if at least it were to deliver him into the hands of God—
To have a child these days,
only to deliver him into the mouth of a cannon,
to abandon him at Sorrow's door,
to cast him on the waters of confusion.
To have a child these days,
only to have him suffer hunger and sun,
and not listen to my voice,
only to learn the catechism later.
To have a child these days,
only to have him blinded with passion
or victim of persecution,
only to witness destruction.
To have a child these days...
I carry him around inside me,
where even he himself cannot hurt him,
where only God can make him die.

—*Kate Flores*

THE BIRDS NEST IN MY ARMS

The birds nest in my arms,
on my shoulders, behind my knees,
between my breasts I have quails,
the birds think I'm a tree.
The swans think I'm a fountain,
they all come down and drink when I talk.
The sheep nudge me going by,
and the sparrows eat from my fingers;
the ants think I'm the earth
and men think I am nothing.

—*Kate Flores*

A UN HOMBRE

Salvar este gran abismo del sexo
y luego todo será sencillo.
Yo podré decirte que soy feliz
o desdichada,
que amo todavía
irrealizables cosas.
Tú me dirás tus secretos de hombre,
tu orfandad ante la vida,
tu miserable grandeza.
Seremos dos hermanos,
dos amigos, dos almas
que alientan por una misma causa.
Hace tiempo que dejé la coquetería
olvidada en el rincón oscuro
y polvoriento
de mi primera, balbuciente, femineidad.
¡Ahora sólo quiero que me des la mano
con la fraternal melancolía
de todos los seres que padecen el mismo destino!
No afiles porque soy mujer
tu desdén o tu galantería,
no me des la limosna
de tu caballerosidad insalvable y amarga.
¡Quiero tu corazón sin amor,
pero amigo! Ese corazón leal
que repartes
entre los seres de tu mismo sexo.
¿No alcanzaremos nunca
la paz de nuestras vidas,
la amistad que hace alta el alma,
calurosa la soledad, alegre el mundo?
Como yo me desnudo
de mis naturales artificios,
desnúdate tú de complejidad,
¡y sé mi amigo!

SUSANA MARCH
(SPAIN, 1918–)

TO A MAN

Overcome this great divide of sex
and everything will be simple.
I will be able to tell you whether I am happy
or wretched,
that I still love
unattainable things.
You will tell me your manly secrets,
your orphanage before life,
your miserable grandeur.
We shall be two brothers,
two friends, two souls
moved by a single cause.
Long ago I discarded the coquettishness,
forgotten in a dark
and dusty corner,
of my first, tremulous femininity.
Now I want you only to hold my hand
with the fraternal sadness
of all human beings enduring the same destiny!
Do not because I am a woman emphasize
your gallantry or your scorn,
do not bestow upon me the alms
of your courtesy insurmountable and bitter.
I want your heart without love,
but with friendship! That loyal heart
which you parcel out
among those of your own sex.
Will we ever attain
peace in our lives,
the friendship which uplifts the soul,
gives warmth to loneliness, happiness to the world?
Just as I rid myself
of my natural artifices,
rid yourself of your complexity,
and be my friend!

—*Kate Flores*

PARA DECIRLO

Qué hijos de una tal por cual
qué bestias
cómo decirlo de otro modo
cómo
qué dedo acusador es suficiente
qué anatema
qué llanto
qué palabra que no sea un insulto
serviría
no para conmoverlos
ni para convencerlos
ni para detenerlos
Sólo para decirlo.

TODO ES MUY SIMPLE

Todo es muy simple mucho
más simple y sin embargo
aun así hay momentos
en que es demasiado para mí
en que no entiendo
y no sé reirme a carcajadas
o si llorar de miedo
o estarme aquí sin llanto
sin risas
en silencio
asumiendo mi vida mi tránsito mi tiempo.

IDEA VILARIÑO
(URUGUAY, 1920–)

IN ORDER TO SAY IT

What sons of so and so
what beasts
how to say it otherwise
how
what accusing finger is enough
what anathema
what weeping
what word that would not be an insult
would serve
not in order to influence them
or to convince them
or to stop them.
Merely in order to say it.

—*Kate Flores*

EVERYTHING IS VERY SIMPLE

Everything is very simple much
more simple and yet
even so there are moments
when it is all too much for me
when I do not understand
and do not know whether to burst out laughing
or weep with fear
or stay here without weeping
without laughter
in silence
feigning my life my passage my time.

—*Kate Flores*

LA SIRENA

Decir no
decir no
atarme al mástil
pero
deseando que el viento lo voltee
que la sirena suba y con los dientes
corte las cuerdas y me arrastre al fondo
diciendo no no no
pero siguiéndola.

NO HAY NADIE

No estoy
no esperes más
hace tiempo me he ido
no busques
no preguntes
no llames que no hay nadie.
Es una loca brisa de otros días
que gime
es un pañuelo al viento
que remeda señales.
No llames
no destroces tu mano
golpeando
no grites no preguntes
que no hay nadie
no hay nadie.

THE SIREN

To say no
to say no
to tie myself to the mast
while
hoping the wind will turn it around
that the siren will climb up and with her teeth
sever the ropes and drag me down to the depths
saying no no no
but following after her.

—*Kate Flores*

THERE'S NOBODY

I am not in
don't wait any longer
I left long ago
do not look
do not ask
do not call for there's nobody here.
It's just a crazy breeze from bygone days
that is sobbing
a handkerchief in the wind
that seems to signal.
Do not call
do not bruise your hand
knocking
do not shout do not ask
for there is nobody
there is nobody.

—*Kate Flores*

EN LA PLAYA

A Carole

No ha sido nada.
Ven.
Recoge el balde con la otra mano
te contaré otro cuento si no lloras
pasa en la China el cuento
¿sabes dónde es la China?
Dijo que no con la cabeza
y se acercó sin ganas
con la nariz mocosa
y el bañador azul
chorreando arena.
Hace mucho, le dije
mientras la sentaba en mi regazo
allá en la China
les ataban los pies a las mujeres
para que no crecieran
todo el resto crecía
sólo el pie
se quedaba allí preso
entre las vendas
y las pobres mujeres
casi no podían caminar
las uñas de las manos
se las dejaban largas
más que uñas eran garras
y las pobres mujeres
apenas si podían levantar una taza
para tomar el té.
No es que fueran inútiles
es que así las querían
sus maridos
sus padres
sus hermanos
un objeto de lujo
o una esclava.
Eso sucede aún
en todo el mundo
no son los pies los que atan
es la mente, Carole

CLARIBEL ALEGRÍA
(NICARAGUA, 1924–)

ON THE BEACH

For Carole

It's really nothing.
Come here.
Pick up the bucket with your other hand
I'll tell you another story if you stop crying
it happened in China
Do you know where China is?
She shakes her head, no,
and approaches reluctantly
with her runny nose
and her blue bathing trunks
shedding sand.
A long time ago, I tell her
as she climbs onto my lap,
far away in China
they used to bind women's feet
so they'd stop growing
all the rest of them grew
except their feet
imprisoned in bandages
and the poor women
could scarcely walk
their fingernails
were left long
more claws than fingernails
and the poor women
could scarcely pick up a cup
to drink their tea.
It's not that they were useless
it's that their fathers
their husbands
their brothers
wanted them that way:
a luxury object
or a slave.
That still happens
all over the world
it's not their feet that are bound
but their minds, Carole,

y hay mujeres que aceptan
y mujeres que no.
Déjame que te cuente
de Rafaela Herrera:
junto a otras mujeres
espantó nada menos
que a Lord Nelson
con tambores
con cohetes
y con gritos
no había ningún hombre
sólo fueron mujeres
tuvo miedo Lord Nelson
creyó que el pueblo entero
se había sublevado
(llegaba de Inglaterra a invadir Nicaragua)
y regresó a su patria
derrotado.
Tu dedito torcido
es como ser mujer
tienes que usarlo mucho
y verás cómo sirve.
Vuelve a jugar ahora
no acarrees arena
ayúdale a tus primos
a construir el castillo
ponle torres
y muros
y terrazas
y destruye
y construye
no acarrees arena
deja que ellos lo hagan
por un rato
que te traigan a ti
baldes de arena.

and there are women who accept it
and women who don't.
Let me tell you about
Rafaela Herrera:
together with other women
she terrified none other
than Lord Nelson
with drums
with fireworks
with shouts
there wasn't a single man there
only women
Lord Nelson was frightened
he thought the whole country
had risen against him
(he'd come from England to invade Nicaragua)
and he returned to his own land
defeated.
Your twisted thumb
is like being a woman
you'll have to use it a lot
and you'll see how well it serves you.
Run along and play now
don't carry sand
help your cousins
build the castle
put towers on it
and walls
and terraces
and knock it down
and build it up
don't carry sand
let them do it
for a while
let them bring you
bucketsful of sand.

—*Darwin J. Flakoll*

CREÍ PASAR MÍ TIEMPO

Creí pasar mi tiempo
amando
y siendo amada
comienzo a darme cuenta
que lo pasé despedazando
mientras era a mi vez
des
    pe
       da
          za
            da.

SE HABLA DE GABRIEL

Como todos los huéspedes mi hijo me estorbaba
ocupando un lugar que era mi lugar,
existiendo a deshora,
haciéndome partir en dos cada bocado.

Fea, enferma, aburrida
lo sentía crecer a mis expensas,
robarle su color a mi sangre, añadir
un peso y un volumen clandestinos
a mi modo de estar sobre la tierra.

Su cuerpo me pidió nacer, cederle el paso;
darle un sitio en el mundo,
la provisión de tiempo necesaria a su historia.

Consentí. Y por la herida en que partió, por esa
hemorragia de su desprendimiento
se fue también lo último que tuve
de soledad, de yo mirando tras de un vidrio.

Quedé abierta, ofrecida
a las visitaciones, al viento, a la presencia.

I THOUGHT TO SPEND MY TIME

I thought to spend my time
loving
and being loved
I'm beginning to realize
that I spent it dismembering
while I was in my turn
dis
   mem
      be
        r
          ed.

—*Darwin J. Flakoll*

ROSARIO CASTELLANOS
(MEXICO, 1925–1974)

SPEAKING OF GABRIEL

Like all visitors my son disturbed me,
taking a place that was my place,
existing unpropitiously,
making me divide every mouthful in two.

Ugly, sick, bored,
I felt him grow at my expense,
steal his color from my blood, add
a weight and a secret breadth
to my own way of being on the earth.

His body begged me to be born, to cede him the way,
to give him a place in the world,
the quota of time essential for his history.

I consented. And when he came through that wound, through that
hemorrhage of dislodgment,
there departed as well the last I had
of solitude, of gazing out from behind a window.

I was left open, receptive
to visitations, to the wind, to presence.

—*Kate Flores*

JORNADA DE LA SOLTERA

Da vergüenza estar sola. El día entero
arde un rubor terrible en su mejilla.
(Pero la otra mejilla está eclipsada.)

La soltera se afana en quehacer de ceniza,
en labores sin mérito y sin fruto;
y a la hora en que los deudos se congregan
alrededor del fuego, del relato,
se escucha el alarido
de una mujer que grita en un páramo inmenso
en el que cada peña, cada tronco
carcomido de incendios, cada rama
retorcida, es un juez
o es un testigo sin misericordia.

De noche la soltera
se tiende sobre el lecho de agonía.
Brota un sudor de angustia a humedecer las sábanas
y el vacío se puebla
de diálogos y hombres inventados.

Y la soltera aguarda, aguarda, aguarda.

Y no puede nacer en su hijo, en sus entrañas,
y no puede morir
en su cuerpo remoto, inexplorado,
planeta que el astrónomo calcula,
que existe aunque no ha visto.

Asomada a un cristal opaco la soltera
—astro extinguido—pinta con un lápiz
en sus labios la sangre que no tiene

Y sonríe ante un amanecer sin nadie.

MEDITACIÓN EN EL UMBRAL

No, no es la solución
tirarse bajo un tren como la Ana de Tolstoy
ni apurar el arsénico de Madame Bovary
ni aguardar en los páramos de Ávila la visita
del ángel con venablo
antes de liarse el manto a la cabeza
y comenzar a actuar.

DAILY ROUND OF THE SPINSTER

To be solitary is shameful. All day long
a terrible blush burnishes her cheek
(while the other is in eclipse).

She busies herself in a labor of ashes,
at tasks worthless and fruitless;
and when her relatives gather
around the fire, telling stories,
the howl is heard
of a woman wailing on a boundless plain
where every boulder, every scorched tree stump,
every twisted bough is a judge
or a witness without mercy.

At night the spinster
stretches herself out on her bed of agony.
An anguished sweat breaks out to dampen the sheets
and the void is peopled
with made-up dialogues and men.

And the spinster waits, waits, waits.

And she cannot be born in her child, in her womb,
nor can she die
in her far-off, unexplored body,
a planet the astronomer can calculate,
existent though unseen.

Peering into a dark mirror the spinster
—extinguished star—paints on her lips
with a lipstick the blood she does not have.

And smiles at a dawn without anyone at all.

—*Kate Flores*

MEDITATION AT THE THRESHOLD

No, the solution is not
to jump beneath a train, like Tolstoy's Anna,
nor to swallow Madame Bovary's arsenic,
nor to wait on the barren plains of Ávila
for the visit of the angel with the javelin
before tying the scarf around one's head
and beginning to act.

Ni concluir las leyes geométricas, contando
las vigas de la celda de castigo
como lo hizo Sor Juana. No es la solución
escribir, mientras llegan las visitas,
en la sala de estar de la familia Austen
ni encerrarse en el ático
de alguna residencia de la Nueva Inglaterra
y soñar, con la Biblia de los Dickinson,
debajo de una almohada de soltera.

Debe haber otro modo que no se llame Safo
ni Messalina ni María Egipcíaca
ni Magdalena ni Clemencia Isaura.

Otro modo de ser humano y libre.

Otro modo de ser.

NO ME RELACIONO

No me relaciono con el desastre
ni con la muerte.
Soy un as-pájaro que come vida
adaptado a diámetros de luna y sol.
Una mujer pacífica en un mundo de batallas.
Hay tanta cólera en la mente de los hombres
Cuándo van a comprender que hay
un camino distinto
para llegar a los grandes poderes?
Porque
qué cosa duradera redime la violencia?
Qué es lo que la sangre lava para siempre?
Si todo queda realmente negro
bajo una costra de tristeza.
Nuestro espíritu no está hecho para matar
y a veces mata
en el nombre moderno de Dios
que es el Dios de las excusas.

Nor to deduce the laws of geometry by counting
the rafters of the castigation cell,
as Sor Juana did. The solution is not
to write, when visitors come
to the living room of the Austin family,
nor to shut oneself up in the attic
of some house in New England
and dream, with the Dickinson Bible
under a maidenly pillow.

There has to be some other way that isn't called Sappho,
or Messalina, or Mary of Egypt,
or Magdalene, or Clementia Isaura.

Another way to be human and free.

Another way to be.

—*Kate Flores*

RAQUEL JODOROWSKY
(CHILE, 1937–)

I DO NOT RELATE

I do not relate to disaster
or to death.
I am a super-bird who feeds on life
adapted to diameters of sun and moon.
A peaceable woman in a world at war.
There is so much anger in men's mentality!
When will they understand
that there is a different way
to reach the great powers?
For
what enduring thing redeems violence?
What is it that blood washes away forever?
If everything actually remains dark
beneath a scar of sadness?
Our spirit is not made for killing
and yet sometimes it kills
in the modern name of God
who is the God of excuses.

Cómo quisiera que esta humanidad no sea
una flor de música destinada a quemarse!
Cómo olvidar las tradiciones, los dráculas
las artes-trampas que dirigen la decapitación
desaparecen ciudades o gobiernan las almas
introduciendo microbios que carcomen
la alegría de vivir.
De suerte que estos errores invaden un siglo
confunden los pueblos y alteran
el movimiento del corazón del hombre.
Hemos olvidado lo grandioso que somos.

Mi poesía siente frío en este mundo
donde no me relaciono con la especie.
...Y mientras ellos caen yo resisto...

EL SECRETO

Ha pasado un siglo.
Un día alguien levantará
una piedra abandonada
para estudiar
el pasado del mundo.
Y ahí debajo, ensombrecido
estará mi poema.
Nadie sabrá repetirlo.
Sobre la tierra, nuevos hombres
nuevos sonidos, nuevos poetas
van trabajando y cantan.
Así mis lágrimas quedarán
en secreto para siempre.
Y yo estaré feliz, con mi pena sólo mía
en un poema que no puede ya contaminar.
Impronunciada, inexistente
Sólo heredando el peso de las piedras...

How could one want this humanity not to be,
a flower of music destined for burning!
How to forget traditions, the draculas,
the subterfuges meant for decapitation!
Cities disappear or govern souls
introducing microbes that gnaw away
at the joy of living.
Thus do these blunders invade a century,
confusing the people and altering
the movement of men's hearts.
We have forgotten the grandeur that we are!

My poetry feels cold in this world
where I do not relate to the species.
...And as it falls I resist...

—*Kate Flores*

SECRET

A century has gone by.
One day someone will lift up
an abandoned stone
in order to study
the world's past.
And down there, in darkness,
will be my poem.
No one will know how to repeat it.
Upon the earth new men,
new sounds, new poets
will be working and singing.
Thus will my tears remain
secret forever.
And I shall be glad, with my sorrow mine alone
in a poem no longer contaminating.
Unpronounced, nonexistent,
Its only legacy the weight of the stones...

—*Kate Flores*

AQUÍ ESTAMOS

Aquí estamos las madres negras
petrificándonos
como un raro ejemplar
de otras edades.
Sin que estas palabras
puedan cambiar
las decisiones de los hombres
que mantienen los pueblos
en la sombra.
Aquí estamos las mujeres poderosas
rodeadas de atormentadores
reducidas a cenizas
por la mano del hombre.
Dónde va a florecer nuestra familia
si se contamina la vida
en el Pacífico
y hacen estallar el espacio
rompen el aire de dragones imaginarios
si desequilibran las nieves de los Polos
y también las profundidades de la tierra?
Dónde alimentar la sonrisa de los hijos
con peces muertos, vegetales muertos, aire muerto
alimento envenenado
cabellos, piel, el color de los ojos
envenenado
la alegría de vivir envenenada.
Sin que ninguna de mis palabras
pueda cambiar nada
Aquí me desintegro
sin haber tomado parte
ni ser poeta comprometida
con cualquiera de estas mentes
destructoras
de mis generaciones sobre la tierra.

HERE WE ARE

Here we are mothers in darkness
petrifying
like a rare specimen
of other ages.
Without these words
being capable of changing
the decisions of the men
who keep the people
in shadows.
Here we are powerful women
surrounded by torturers
reduced to ashes
by the hand of man.
Where can our families flourish
if life is contaminated
in the Pacific
if space is blown up
the air sundered by imaginary dragons,
if the snows at the Poles
as well as the entrails of the earth
are in disequilibrium?
How can we nourish the smiles of our children
with dead fish, dead vegetables, dead air,
poisoned food,
hair, skin, the color of their eyes
poisoned,
their joy in life poisoned?
With no words of mine
able to change anything
Here I disintegrate
having taken no part
nor been a poet compromised
in any way whatever by these minds
destructive
of my generations on the earth.

—*Kate Flores*

EL HOMBRE ES UN ANIMAL QUE RÍE

El hombre es un animal que ríe
o es un animal que llora
pero cuándo es
un hombre qué piensa?
Pues así como vamos
harán de este mundo
la arquitectura del fin.
Los partidos políticos
que levantan pedestales
de un movimiento sí y de otro no
¡Poetas tuertos!
Lo importante es abarcar el mundo
de esta parte y de la otra
de la ira y del amor
y tragarse la verdad de sus mentiras
y las mentiras de su verdad.
No la vida dividida
a la derecha y a la izquierda
sino la totalidad del sudor
la unidad del esfuerzo
Reunido.
Déjennos al menos un tiempo
hombrecitos rabiosos
jefes de las banderas
sentar sobre sus cerebros marchitos
nuestros sexos bellos
déjennos romper las riendas de los pueblos
para que se desboquen
como caballos felices por la tierra

MAN IS AN ANIMAL THAT LAUGHS

Man is an animal that laughs
or an animal that weeps
but when is he
a man who thinks?
For the way we are going
they will make of this world
the architecture of the end.
The political parties
that set up pedestals
crown man
with a yes movement and a no movement.
One-eyed poets!
What is important is to embrace the world
from this side as well as from the other,
with wrath and with love,
and to swallow the truth of its lies
and the lies of its truth.
Not life divided into right and left
but the totality of sweat,
the unity of reunited effort.
Allow us at least for a while,
little madmen,
chiefs of the flags,
to place our beautiful sex
astride your withered brains
allow us to undo the harnesses of the people
that they may run loose
like happy horses across the earth.

—*Kate Flores*

LA ÚNICA MUJER

La única mujer que puede ser
es la que sabe que el sol para su vida empieza ahora

la que no derrama lágrimas sino dardos para
sembrar la alambrada de su territorio

la que no comete ruegos
la que opina y levanta su cabeza y agita su cuerpo
y es tierna sin vergüenza y dura sin odios

la que desaprende el alfabeto de la sumisión
y camina erguida
la que no le teme a la soledad porque siempre ha estado sola
la que deja pasar los alaridos grotescos de la violencia
y la ejecuta con gracia
la que se libera en el amor pleno
la que ama

la única mujer que puede ser la única
es la que dolorida y limpia decide por sí misma
salir de su prehistoria

PENA TAN GRANDE

Con mi pena tan grande
salí a buscar la compasión ajena

a mi paso tropecé con la vecina
del tercer piso que vive sola y
da de comer y de vestir a cuatro hijos
y fue despedida de su trabajo
porque no cumple el horario completo

su hijo mayor de nueve años
debe ser tratado por un especialista
para ''niños excepcionales''

BERTALICIA PERALTA
(PANAMA, 1939–)

THE ONLY WOMAN

The only woman who is able to be
is she who knows that the dawn of her life begins now

she who marks out her own domain
not with tears but with arrows

who resorts to no prayers
who states opinions and lifts her head and moves her body
and is tender without shame and tough without hatred

she who has unlearned the alphabet of obedience
and walks erect
who does not fear solitude because she has always been solitary
she who forgoes grotesque howls of violence
uttering them rather with grace
she who frees herself in bounteous love
she who loves

the only woman who can be one
is she who sadly and simply decides on her own
to emerge from her past history

—Kate Flores

SO MUCH SUFFERING

With so much suffering
I went out to seek sympathy

on the way I met my neighbor
who lives on the third floor alone and
feeds and clothes four kids
and was fired from her job
because she could not keep her schedule

her oldest son, nine years old,
has to be treated by a specialist
in "exceptional children"

y a ella le cansan las caminatas por
las várices de sus piernas

casi mi indigesto de vergüenza
por mi pena tan grande

TANGO

Soy esa borrachera que necesitás a mitad de año
cuando el aguinaldo
las vacaciones
el ascenso
aún están lejos
soy la nota disonante
que te ayuda a sobrellevar esa armonía monótona
que decís que es tu vida
soy ese minuto de locura
que te permite aguantar el resto de la hora
el elogio dicho con firmeza tal que descarta tu duda
la urna en que depositás tus lastimeros "vos no sabés"
tus pequeñas frustraciones cotidianas
tus:
el café está frío
quién me abrió esta carta
otra vez la cuenta del gas

soy la que despierta los rincones más inéditos de tu piel
la que te hace decir:
con vos me siento otra vez un colegial

soy
en otras palabras
esa mujer que te llevás a un hotel
en una noche de borrachera
y a quien te olvidás de preguntar su nombre
o si podrás volver a verla algún día.

and the long walk tires her out because
she has varicose veins in her legs

I am overcome with shame
that I suffer so much

—*Robert L. Smith and Judith Cundullo*

ELENA JORDANA
(ARGENTINA, 1940–)

TANGO

I am the binge you need
midway through the year
when your bonus
your vacation
your raise
are still far off
I am the discordant note
that helps you bear the monotonous harmony
you call your life
I am the momentary folly
that lets you endure the rest of the hour
the praise so sure it dispels your doubts
the container that holds your petulant "you just don't understands"
your petty everyday frustrations
your:
the-coffee-is-cold
who's-been-opening-my-mail?
it's-the-gasbill-again

I am the one who rouses the most unexpected depths of your skin
the one who makes you say:
you make me feel like a schoolboy again

I am
in short
the woman you take to a hotel
on a drunken night
and forget to ask her name
or whether some day you can see her again.

—*William M. Davis*

ENVÍO

a mi madre, y a la estatua de mi madre,
a mis tías, y a sus modales exquisitos,
a Marta, así como también María,
porque supo escoger la mejor parte.
a Francesca, la inmortal, porque desde su infierno insiste
en cantarle al amor y a la agonía,
a Catalina, que deslaza sobre el agua
las obscenidades más prístinas de su éxtasis
únicamente cuando silba el hacha,
a Rosario, y a la sombra de Rosario,
a las erinnias y a las furias que entablaron
junto a su cuna el duelo y la porfía,
a todas las que juntas accedieron
a lo que también consentí,
dedico el cumplimento de estos versos:
porque canto,
porque coso y brillo y limpio y aún me duelen
los huesos musicales de mi alma,
porque lloro y escribo en una copa
el jugo natural de mi experiencia,
me declaro hoy enemiga de ese exánime
golpe de mi mano airada
con que vengo mi desdicha y mi destino.
porque amo,
porque vivo, y soy mujer, y no me animo
a amordazar sin compasión a mi conciencia,
porque río y cumplo y plancho entre nosotras
los mínimos dobleces de mi caos,
me declaro hoy a favor del gozo y de la gloria.

ROSARIO FERRÉ
(PUERTO RICO, 1940–)

ENVOI

to my mother, and to my mother's monument,
to my aunts, and to their well-bred manners,
to Martha, as well as to Mary,
because she dared to choose the better part.
to Francesca, the immortal one, because from the deepest hell
she insists on praising love and agony,
to Catherine, who unravels over water
the pristine obscenities of her ecstasy
each time she strums the axes' whistle,
to Rosario, and to Rosario's shadow,
to the Erinyes and the Furies who, locked in amorous strife,
mourned and sang over her cradle,
to all those who agreed in principle
to what I also consented to,
I address the completion of these verses:
because I sing,
because I still sew and shine and rearrange
the ever-changing order of my bones,
because I cry and trace, o'er my goblet's vanished breath
the humors of my human-borne experience,
I declare myself the mortal foe
of my own hand's irate, harmless blow
as I avenge my destiny's misfortune.
because I love,
because I still live, and am, and hesitate to gag
my hardheaded woman's side,
because I still laugh, and keep my promises, and mercilessly
iron, amongst all of us, the tiniest creases of my chaos,
I confirm today my right to joy and glory.

—*Rosario Ferré*

VIRGINIA WOOLF, ETC.

Virginia Woolf, etc.
dulces antepasadas mías
ahogándose en el mar
o suicidadas en jardines imaginarios
encerradas en castillos de muros lilas
y arrogantes
espléndidas en su desafío
a la biología elemental
que hace de una mujer una paridera
antes de ser en realidad una mujer
soberbias de soledad y en el pequeño escándalo
de sus vidas
tienen lugar en el herbolario
junto a los ejemplares raros
de diversas nervadura.

MIENTRAS TÚ

Mientras tú
llegas a casa,
abres una cerveza
observas la televisión
mientras tú
te acomodas en tu sillón de siempre
comentas lo duro que se pasa en la oficina
ocultas las veces que le propusiste a la
    secretaria una cita
las veces que con tus compañeros en el cafe
    piropeaste a las mujeres
mientras tú
decides a cuál bar irás hoy

CRISTINA PERI ROSSI
(URUGUAY, 1941–)

VIRGINIA WOOLF, ETC.

Virginia Woolf, etc.,
sweet foremothers of mine
drowning in the sea
or committing suicide in imaginary gardens
locked up in castles with lilac-colored
arrogant walls
splendid women challenging
the elemental biology
which reduces women to parturition machines
before being really women
superb in solitude and in the little scandal
of their lives
they have a place in the herbarium
beside the rare specimens
of variegated nervure.

—*Kate Flores*

BESSY REYNA
(PANAMA, 1942–)

WHILE YOU

While you
come home
open a beer
and watch TV
while you
settle down in the same old chair
and say how tough things are at the office
you don't say how often you
    asked the secretary for a date
how often you and your drinking pals
    made passes at the girls in the bar
while you
decide what café you'll head for today

o te sumerges en el comercial y esperas la cena
ella
trata de olvidarse de los piropos de mal gusto
que soportó camino al trabajo
de las proposiciones del jefe y los clientes
ella
trata de preparar la cena
arreglar la casa
sonreír a los niños
y pretender que tus escapadas
son un juego pasajero
que tus caprichos son un juego pasajero
y que a pesar de todo ella es una
   señora feliz.

MUJER NEGRA

Todavía huelo la espuma del mar que me hicieron atravesar.
La noche, no puedo recordarla.
Ni el mismo océano podría recordarla.
Pero no olvido al primer alcatraz que divisé.
Altas, las nubes, como inocentes testigos presenciales.
Acaso no he olvidado ni mi costa perdida, ni mi lengua ancestral.
Me dejaron aquí y aquí he vivido.
Y porque trabajé como una bestia,
aquí volví a nacer.
A cuánta epopeya mandinga intenté recurrir.

Me rebelé.

Su Merced me compró en una plaza.
Bordé la casaca de Su Merced y un hijo macho le parí.
Mi hijo no tuvo nombre.
Y Su Merced murió a manos de un impecable *lord* inglés.

Anduve.

or submerge in the commercial and wait for dinner
she
tries to forget the tasteless flirting
she put up with on her way to work
how she was propositioned by the customers and by the boss
she
tries to prepare dinner
fix up the house
smile at the kids
and tell herself that your escapades
are just a passing fancy
that your whims are just a passing notion
and that she in spite of everything is
   a happily married woman.

—*William M. Davis*

NANCY MOREJÓN
(CUBA, 1944–)

BLACK WOMAN

I can still smell the spray of the sea they forced me to cross.
But I cannot remember the night.
Not even the ocean could remember it.
But I have not forgotten the first seagull I sighted on the horizon.
The clouds so high, like innocent witnesses.
Perhaps I have not really forgotten my lost coastline, nor
my ancestral tongue.
They left me here and here I have lived.
And because I worked like a beast,
here I was re-born.
Many were the Mandinga epics I turned to for refuge.

           I rebelled.

His Grace bought me in the public square.
I embroidered His Grace's frockcoat and bore Him a male child.
My son had no name.
And His Grace died at the hands of an impeccable English lord.

           I walked.

Ésta es la tierra donde padecí bocabajos y azotes.
Bogué a lo largo de todos sus ríos.
Bajo su sol sembré, recolecté y las cosechas no comí.
Por casa tuve un barracón.
Yo misma traje piedras para edificarlo,
pero canté al natural compás de los pájaros nacionales.

Me sublevé.

En esta misma tierra toqué la sangre húmeda
y los huesos podridos de muchos otros,
traídos a ella, o no, igual que yo.
Ya nunca más imaginé el camino a Guinea.
¿Era a Guinea? ¿A Benín? ¿Era a Madagascar? ¿O a Cabo Verde?

Trabajé mucho más.

Fundé mejor mi canto milenario y mi esperanza.
Aquí construí mi mundo.

Me fui al monte.

Mi real independencia fue el palenque
y cabalgué entre las tropas de Maceo.

Sólo un siglo más tarde,
junto a mis descendientes,
desde una azul montaña,

bajé de la Sierra

para acabar con capitales y usureros,
con generales y burgueses.
Ahora soy: sólo hoy tenemos y creamos.
Nada nos es ajeno.
Nuestra la tierra.
Nuestros el mar y el cielo.
Nuestras la magia y la quimera.
Iguales míos, aquí los veo bailar
alrededor del árbol que plantamos para el comunismo.
Su pródiga madera ya resuena.

This is the land where I suffered the lash with my mouth to the
    ground.
I rowed the length of all its rivers.
Beneath its sun I planted, I reaped, and I did not eat the harvest.
For a home I had the slave barracks.
I myself carried the stones to build it,
but I sang to the natural rhythm of the native birds.

                    I revolted.

In this very land I touched the wet blood
and the rotting bones of many others
brought here, or not, just as I was.
And no longer kept thinking of the road to Guinea.
Was it Guinea? Or Benin? Was it Madagascar? Or Cape Verde?

                    I worked still harder.

I strengthened my song for the millennium and my hope.
Here I constructed my world.

                    I fled to the mountains.

My real independence was the stockade
and I rode with Maceo's troops.

Only a century later,
with my children's children,
from a blue mountain peak

                    I came down from the Sierra

to put an end to capitalists and usurers,
generals and bourgeois.
Now I exist: only today do we have and create.
Nothing is alien to us.
Ours is the land.
Ours the sea and the sky.
Ours the magic and the dream.
Here I see dancing all my equals
around the tree we planted for communism.
Already its prolific wood resounds.

—Lisa E. Davis

MARÍA ENCADENADA

(A una niña, mientras le taladran los oídos)

Llora, pequeña.
Te están circuncidando la belleza,
                        llora,
tus tenues agujeros de esclava
pregonarán tu rol desde la sangre.
Te están atando al oro
                    para que no recuerdes
ni voluntad ni inteligencia,
para que seas eternamente la muñeca
presa de adornos y miradas.
Tus dos pétalos de rosa taladrados
son el primer dolor de tu recuerdo,
                        llora,
te espera una isla de vestidos
donde cada deseo te mojará las alas.
Un paraíso de espejos,
                    de tules y de encajes
te da la bienvenida,
tu mañana tendrá el color del maquillaje.
Los focos, las joyas y las fiestas
                    con sus mil tentáculos
matarán tu tiempo atenazado.
Sonreirás
la sumisión standard que te marquen
en el mundo consumo de los sexos.

JUANA CASTRO
(SPAIN, 1945–)

MARIA ENCHAINED

(To a little girl having her ears pierced)

Cry, little one,
while they circumcise your beauty,
                                        cry
while in your tender earlobes
they stamp your servitude in blood.
They will bind you in chains of gold
                        to make you forget
you have a mind and a will,
to make you a doll
forever entrapped in ornament and show.
Your two punctured rose petals
will be the first pain you remember,
                                        cry,
an island of gowns awaits you
where everyone's wishes will dampen your wings.
A paradise of mirrors,
                        of tulle and of lace
is to welcome you,
and all your days will be daubed with makeup.
Lights, jewels and parties,
                        with their thousand tentacles
will kill your curlered time.
And you will smile
the standard submissiveness with which they brand you
in the buyer's market of the sexes.

—*Kate Flores*

LA MUJER IDEAL

Desde hace cincuenta años
se ha estado eligiendo en Inglaterra
La Mujer Ideal.
Cada año incontables jovencitas
concursan en los siguientes rubros:
Elegancia
Rapidez de Arreglo
Belleza
Arte de Cocinar
Arte de Planchar.
La más bella y diligente
obtiene el título.

Otros estudiosos han dedicado
su vida a observar los destinos
de las cincuenta Mujeres Ideales
que lucían tan bellas y normales
durante el concurso.

Se llegó a la conclusión
de que treinta de ellas
se habían convertido en alcohólicas,
diez en drogadictas
y otras diez en Dueñas de Casa
relativamente infelices:

Marie Jose Berlant: después de algunos años
de vagabundaje sexual
casó con un Conde Mayor,
se hizo alcohólica
y hoy descansa
en un asilo de ancianas.

Juana Mardoquí: felizmente enamorada
casó con un profesional,
fueron muy felices
hasta que él se suicidó
y ella gastó los últimos años
de juventud en el amor.

CECILIA VICUÑA
(CHILE, 1948–)

THE IDEAL WOMAN

Every year for the last fifty
the Ideal Woman
has been elected
in England.
Every year innumerable young ladies
compete in the following categories:
Elegance
Cosmetic Art
Beauty
Culinary Art
The Art of Ironing.
The most beautiful—
and diligent—
wins the title.

Certain scientists
have dedicated
a lifetime to a study of the subsequent careers
of those wholesome beauties
displayed on the runway:
the fifty Ideal Women.

The results?
Alcoholics—30
Drug Addicts—10
Relatively Miserable Housewives—10

Anne-Marie Venture: after some years
                  of sexual vagabondage
                  she married a title,
                  took to drink
                  and now resides
                  in a nursing home.

Fatima Mardoqui: lucky in love,
                  she married a professional man;
                  they were the perfect couple
                  until he killed himself
                  and she spent the last years
                  of her youth going from one man
                  to the next.

Jovita Desmanes: aficionóse a viajar,
después de varias ofertas,
optó por la soltería.
Dicen que la heroína
fue su única fiel compañía.

Estrella Martínez: visiblemente extrovertida,
alcanzó notoriedad nacional.
La excesiva alegría
dió con ella al fondo
de un canal,
al que se dirigía a toda velocidad
en su Mercedes tapizado de jaguar.

de CANTO AL NUEVO TIEMPO

a mis hermanos del FSLN
a Tomás, que sobrevivió para verlo

Me levanto
yo,
mujer sandinista,
renegada de mi clase,
engendrada entre suaves almohadas
y aposentos iluminados;
sorprendida a los 20 años
por una realidad
lejana a mis vestidos de tules y lentejuelas,
volcada a la ideología de los sin pan y sin tierra,
morenos forjadores de la riqueza,
hombres y mujeres sin más fortuna que su vigor
y sus bruscos movimientos.

Me levanto a cantar
sobre los terremotos
y las voces chillonas, desesperadas,

Luisa Extravaganza: she loved to travel
and, after various offers,
chose the single life.
They say that heroin
was her only faithful companion.

Baby O'Reilly: an eye-catching extrovert,
she won national notoriety.
Youthful exuberance
took her straight to the bottom
of a canal,
reaching it full speed
in her Mercedes upholstered in jaguar.

—*Anne Twitty*

GIOCONDA BELLI
(NICARAGUA, 1948–)

from SONG TO THE NEW DAY

to my brothers of the FSLN
to Tomás, who lived to see it

I rise up
I
a Sandinist woman,
renegade of my class,
begotten between soft pillows
in well-lighted alcoves;
caught up at the age of twenty
by a reality
far removed from my gowns of tulle and spangles,
erupted to the ideology of the breadless and landless,
swarthy forgers of riches,
men and women with no fortune but their strength
and their crude gestures.

I rise up to sing
above the earthquakes
and the strident, desperate voices

de algunos de mis parientes,
reclamando sus por siempre perdidos derechos,
rabiosos ante los desposeídos
que han invadido plazas, teatros, clubes, escuelas,
y que ahora se desplazan, pobres aún,
pero dueños de su Patria y su destino,
orgullosos entre los orgullosos,
volcanes emergiendo del magma de la guerra
árboles crecidos en el fragor de la tormenta.

Me levanto
sobre el cansancio del trabajo,
sobre los muertos que aún viven entre nosotros,
con los que nunca mueren,
hacia la cumbre de la montaña,
desnudando mi apellido, mi nombre,
abandonándolo entre los matorrales,
soltándome de ropas, de despojos brillantes,
para atisbar el horizonte infinito
de la clarinera madrugada de los trabajadores,
que van haciendo los caminos
con sus azadones y machetes y palas,
atronando el día con las rotas cadenas de los siglos
dejadas caer a sus espaldas,
y las mujeres con sus faldas de maíz
—todos los ríos sueltos en sus brazos—
acunando a los niños venidos al tiempo de la esperanza,
niños que dejaron atrás la orfandad de los ranchos destruídos
y los padres asesinados...

Canto,
Cantemos,
para que no se detenga jamás el sonido de estos pasos estallando,
haciendo trizas el pasado,
el brillo de las bayonetas bordeando las fronteras
como una muralla de madres protectoras,
celosamente cuidando a su criatura.
Que manen de la tierra los frutos fértiles
de estos hermosos campos
y resplandezcan las máquinas
trabajando a todo vapor en las fábricas
y salga el sol deparpajado
rompiendo aberturas de puertas y ventanas,
para que tomemos de las crines al tiempo
—alumbre de vientos que barran la miseria—
hombres, mujeres, nacidos con el futuro en andas;

of some of my relatives,
calling for their forever-lost rights,
enraged before the dispossessed
who have invaded the plazas, the theatres, the clubs, the schools,
and who now take over, still poor
but masters of their country and their fate,
proud among the proud ones,
volcanoes emerging from the magma of war
trees arisen amid the clamor of the storm.

I rise up
above the exhaustion of the task,
above the dead ones who still live among us,
with those who never die,
toward the peak of the mountain,
stripping myself of my surname, of my name,
abandoning it in the bushes,
discarding my clothes, my glamorous spoils,
to watch the infinite horizon
of the bugler awaking the workers,
who are going to build roads
with their hoes and machetes and shovels,
thundering the day with the breaking of the chains of the centuries
now fallen from their backs,
and the women with their skirts of corn
—all the rivers loose in their arms—
cradling the children born in the time of hope,
children who have left behind the orphanage of demolished huts
and their murdered parents...

I sing.
Let us sing,
that the sound of these explosive steps may never stop,
shattering to smithereens the past,
the glitter of the bayonets standing at the frontiers,
like a wall of protecting mothers,
jealously guarding their infants.
May abundant crops issue from the earth
of these beautiful fields
and may the machines glisten
as they function fullspeed in the factories
and may the sun rise boldly, breaking through windows and doors,
so that we may seize time by its mane
—shedding light on winds that sweep poverty away—
men, women, bearing the future aloft;
may poetry and love triumph and prosperity arrive,

que triunfe la poesía, el amor y venga la bonanza,
la tapisca del oro y las mazorcas,
la cosecha de palabra y ejemplo,
el trueno decidiendo a los inciertos....

CONTRADICCIONES IDEOLÓGICAS AL LAVAR UN PLATO

¿Entre el Yin y el Yang cuántos eones?
                    —Julio Cortázar

Contradicciones ideológicas al lavar un plato. ¿No?
Y también quisiera explicar
por qué me maquillo y por qué uso perfume.
Por qué quiero cantar la belleza del cuerpo masculino.
Quiero aclararme bien ese racismo que existe
entre los hombres y las mujeres.

Aclararme por qué cuando lavo un plato
o coso un botón
él no ha de estar haciendo lo mismo.
Me pinto el ojo
no por automatismo imbécil
sino porque es el único instante en el día
en que regreso a tiempos ajenos y
mi mano se vuelve egipcia y
el rasgo del ojo, se me queda en la Historia.
La sombra en el párpado me embalsama eternamente
como mujer.
Es el rito ancestral del payaso:
mejillas rojas y boca de color.
Me pinto porque así me dignifico como bufón.
Estoy repitiendo/continuando un acto primitivo.
Es como pintar búfalos en la roca.
Y ya no hay cuevas ni búfalos
pero tengo un cuerpo para texturizarlo a mi gusto.
Uso perfume no porque lo anuncie
Catherine Deneuve o lo use la Bardot
sino porque padezco la enfermedad
del siglo XX, la compulsión de la posesión.
Creer que en una botella puede reposar

abundance of gold and ears of corn,
harvest of words and deeds,
thunder forcing the undecided to decide....

—*Ángel Flores*

KYRA GALVÁN
(MEXICO, 1956–)

IDEOLOGICAL CONTRADICTIONS IN WASHING A DISH

Between yin and yang, how many eons?
                    —Julio Cortázar

Ideological contradictions in washing a dish. Oh, no?
And I would also like to explain
why I make up my face and why I use perfume.
Why I want to sing the beauty of the male body.
I want to clarify to myself this racism that exists
between men and women.

To clarify to myself why when I wash a dish
or sew on a button
he does not have to be doing the same thing.
I paint my eyes
not out of imbecile automatism
but because it is the only moment of the day
that I return to ancient times and
my hand becomes Egyptian and
the shape of my eyes places me in History.
My eyeshadow embalms me eternally
as woman.
It is the ancestral rite of the clown:
red cheeks and colored mouth.
I paint myself thus to dignify myself as buffoon.
I am repeating/continuing a primitive act.
It is like painting buffaloes on the rocks.
And although there are no caves or buffaloes any more
I have a body to texturize to my taste.
I use perfume not because it is advertised
by Catherine Deneuve or Bardot uses it
but rather because I suffer the sickness
of the 20th century: the need to possess.
Believing that in a bottle there can repose

toda la magia del cosmos,
que me voy a quitar de encima
el olor de la herencia,
la gravedad de la crisis capitalista,
porque a pesar de todo/hembra
Se dice que las mujeres débiles/que los hombres fuertes.
Sí y nuestras *razas* tan distintas.
Nuestros sexos tan diversamente complementarios.
Yin & Yang.
La otra parte es el misterio que nunca desnudaremos.
Nunca podré saber—y lo quisiera—
qué se siente estar enfundada en un cuerpo masculino
y ellos no sabrán lo que es olerse a mujer
tener cólicos y jaquecas y
todas esas prendas que solemos usar.
Dos universos físicos en dialéctica constante
con la nostalgia de una unión duradera
donde la fusión de los dos desconocidos
llegue a la profundidad del entendimiento.
Hay una necesidad compulsiva
de dar razones para la escisión
para agudizar racismos con sonrisas
Y las amigas   y los amigos
                ellos comprenderán
Ellos entienden la distancia que te separa
del amigo/amado/enemigo/desconocido.
        Que la reconciliación es un esfuerzo máximo.
La unión, la sublimación
        de nuestros propios misterios.
Que el lavar un plato
significa a veces afirmar
las contradicciones de clase
                entre el hombre y la mujer.

all the magic of the cosmos,
that I am going to rid myself forthwith
of the smell of my heredity,
of the gravity of the capitalist crisis,
because I am above all/female.
They say that women are weak/men strong.
Yes and our *races* are so distinct.
Our sexes so variously complementary.
Yin & yang.
On the other hand is the mystery we will never uncover.
I shall never be able to know — and I should like to —
what it is like to be encased in a masculine body
and they will never know what it is to smell like a woman
to have cramps and headaches and
all that jewelry we are accustomed to wearing.
Two physical universes in constant dialectic
with the nostalgia for a durable union
where the fusion of two unknowns
reaches the depth of understanding.
There is a compulsive need
to give reasons for the schism
to sharpen racisms with smiles
And girlfriends   and boyfriends
              they will comprehend
They will understand the distance that separates you
from friend/lover/enemy/stranger.
        That reconciliation is a maximum effort.
The union, the sublimation
      of our innate mysteries.
That washing a dish
means at times to affirm
the contradictions of class
        between man and woman.

—Kate Flores

NOTES ON THE POETS

Delmira Agustini (Uruguay, 1886–1914)
The precocious, pampered child of a well-to-do Montevidean family of mixed French, German, Argentine, and Uruguayan lineage, Delmira Agustini attended no schools but was privately educated. Her brief career as a poet began with *El libro blanco* (1907) and included *Cantos de la mañana* (1910) and *Las cálices vacíos* (1913). Agustini was tormented by her longing for an ideal love, which she thought would produce a new human race but decided was unattainable because of the contrast between male and female passion, the one predatory and brutal, the other aesthetic and intellectual.

She died at age twenty-seven, murdered by her estranged husband, whom she had left after a few weeks of marriage.

Claribel Alegría (Nicaragua, 1924–)
Born in Estelí, Nicaragua, Claribel Alegría has published ten books of poems: *Anillo de silencio* (1948), *Suite* (1951), *Vivilia* (1953), *Acuario* (1955), *Huésped de mi tiempo* (1961), *Vía única* (1965), *Aprendizaje* (1970), *Pagaré a cobrar* (1973), *Sobrevivo* (1978)—awarded the Casa de las Américas prize—and *Flowers from the Volcano*, published in a bilingual edition in 1982. *Flowers from the Volcano* describes the demoralization, exile, tortures, destruction, and death wrought by war and dictatorship, all against a background of tropical flora, dank prison cells, and human callousness. In 1984, Alegría joined with other Latin American intellectuals in a peace vigil when military units of the United States and Honduras conducted exercises on the El Salvador/Honduras border.

Alegría has published stories for children, *Tres cuentos* (1958), and a novella, *El detén* (1977). In collaboration with her husband, Darwin J. Flakoll, she published the novel *Cenizas de Izalco* (1966), and in 1984 *Para romper el silencio: Resistencia y lucha en las cárceles salvadoreñas*. They have also edited two anthologies, *New Voices of Hispanic America* (1962) and *Cien poemas de Robert Graves* (1981). Alegría's critical essay *La encrucijada salvadoreña* has received wide circulation throughout Latin America.

Marçia Belisarda (Sor María de Santa Isabel) (Spain, ?–1647)
Marçia Belisarda, as Sor María de Santa Isabel signed her writings, was one of the most prolific women poets of the Spanish Golden Age. Because of frustrated love affairs (a recurrent theme in her poetry), she entered the Real Convento de la Concepción of Toledo, the city of her birth, where she composed religious poems as well as ardent, inspired, and often fa-

cetious, profane ones. Her "Romanze melancólico" expressed plaintive longings for life outside the convent walls. Although her poems were collected and ready for the printer, they were never published. Seventy-eight pages are preserved in Madrid in the Biblioteca Nacional, including these stanzas in reply to a male poet who complained of women's fickleness, a subject which years later inspired the Mexican poet Sor Juana Inés de la Cruz.

Gioconda Belli (Nicaragua, 1948–)
Gioconda Belli began publishing her poetry in magazines and newspapers in 1970. In 1972 she received the Mariano Fiallos Gil Poetry Prize of the Universidad Nacional Autónoma of Nicaragua. By the time her first book of poems, *Sobre la grana* (1974), appeared she had to go into exile in Costa Rica. Her second, *Línea de fuego* (1978), won the Casa de las Américas Prize. Her most recent volume is *Truenos y arco-iris* (1982). Belli coedits the newspaper *Barricada* in Managua and produces cultural programs for television.

Julia de Burgos (Puerto Rico, 1914–1958)
Julia de Burgos grew up without formal education among the campesinos of the Puerto Rican Carolina farmlands. As a young, militant member of the Nationalist party, she wrote newspaper articles advocating Puerto Rican independence and defending workers, women, and blacks. Shortly after divorce ended her first marriage, she published two collections of poems, *Poema en siete surcos* (1938) and *Canción de la verdad* (1939). She left Puerto Rico for Cuba, in a turbulent love affair with a man she always referred to as X, who abused and even tortured her. After escaping from that affair, she married again in New York City, where from 1942 to her death she led a miserable life. One morning in 1958 she was found lying on the sidewalk at Fifth Avenue and 105 Street. Rushed to a hospital, she was registered as a "teacher and professional writer," but hours later this was changed to "amnesiac." To save her from potter's field, friends had her body sent to Puerto Rico. Her posthumous *Obra poética* contains all her poetry.

Rosario Castellanos (Mexico, 1925–1974)
Rosario Castellanos spent her youth in Comitán, in Chiapas state, near the Guatemalan frontier. There, she tells us, "most of the people are Indians who speak only dialects derived from the Maya. The landholdings as well as the customs and traditions are almost the same as those established by the Spaniards at the time of the Conquest." With agrarian reform, however, landlords like her parents were forced to emigrate. They moved to Mexico City where Castellanos had to adjust to new living conditions. Since literature was not a practical vocation, she explored the possibilities of a career in chemistry, then law, but after an exciting political

campaign decided upon philosophy. She received her M.A. at the University of Mexico with a brilliant thesis showing the existence of a genuinely feminine culture. After studying aesthetics at the University of Madrid and traveling extensively in Europe, she returned to Mexico to become the organizer and moving spirit of the Instituto de Ciencias y Artes de Chiapas, in Tuxtla Gutiérrez.

During this time, Castellanos also published small books of verse and also tried her hand at comedies and short stories. Her novel *Balún-Canán* (1957), awarded the Premio Chiapas in 1958 and translated into French, English, and German, and her sketches *Ciudad Real* (1960), depicted Indian life in Chiapas, as did two other novels, *Oficio de tinieblas* (1962), translated into several languages, including Polish, and *Los convidados de agosto* (1964). In 1972 she collected most of the poems written since 1948 in *Poesía eres tu* (*Poetry Is You*), which placed her among the foremost poets of the Hispanic world. Castellanos was electrocuted in a freak accident while serving as Mexican ambassador to Israel.

Juana Castro (Spain, 1945–)

In an autobiographical note written in 1978, Juana Castro declared: "I was born in Villanueva de Córdoba during the years of the famine....In a landscape of nuns and peasants I studied pedagogy, always inhaling the grief of these women, a grief far deeper than that of the scorched and desolate countryside....In my book of poems *Cóncava mujer* (1978) I wept for all these women, harboring the hope that some day we women will find a place side by side with men." According to a letter of October 25, 1983, Castro now resides in Córdoba, where "the children I teach arrange with me concerts of words and drawings, of seasons and music." Two other collections of her poems are *Del dolor y las olas* (1981) and *Paranoia en otoño* (1983), which won the coveted Juan Alcaide prize.

Rosalía de Castro (Spain, 1837–1885)

Registered as of "padres incognitos," Rosalía de Castro was the daughter of Teresa de Castro y Abadía, member of a genteel Galician family, and José Martínez Viojo, believed to be a seminarian, later chaplain of Iria. In accordance with a Portuguese-Galician custom called *amadigo*, whereby upper-class children were farmed out with peasant families and reclaimed at maturity, she was brought up in the country among people who taught her the songs and lore of Galicia. She thus had the advantage of two contrasting cultures, for in 1850 her mother brought her to Santiago de Compostela, where she was given a traditional female education, including music, French, and drawing. She never forgot her origins, however, and felt ostracized all her life by "the deadly poison I carry within me."

In 1857, her slim volume of romantic poems, *La flor* (*The Flower*), was published in Madrid and favorably reviewed by Manuel Murguía, a compatriot whom she married the following year. Moving to various cities in different parts of Spain, and suffering the usual extreme homesickness of Galician exiles, she was repelled by the barrenness of the Castilian landscape and the contempt accorded Galician servants.

Returning to Santiago in 1859, she gave birth to the first of six children, only three of whom survived her. Poorly treated by her husband, she suffered poverty and ill health, and anguished over the plight of women writers. "Women should drop their pens and keep busy darning their husbands' socks," she notes in her sardonic "Literary Women" (1856); "and if they have no husband, then those of their servants." For men think "a talented woman a veritable calamity and would rather marry the ass of Balaam than a bright girl." She expressed similar sentiments in the little-known "Lieders" (1858), an excerpt from one of which is translated here for the first time, as well as in her three novels: *La hija del mar* (*Daughter of the Sea*, 1858), *Flavio* (1861), and *El caballero de botas azules* (*The Gentleman with the Blue Boots*, 1867). In defense of her "temerity" in publishing her first novel she quoted Sappho, St. Teresa, Mme. de Staël, George Sand, Malebranche, and Feijoo.

Rosalía de Castro wrote two books of Galician poems: *Cantares gallegos* (1863) and *Follas novas* (*New Leaves*, 1880), both suffused with the sadness and beauty of her province, one of Spain's poorest and loveliest, and with sympathy for its downtrodden people, especially its women, often left alone as the men had to seek work abroad. Two of these poems are translated here for the first time: "Today black hair" and "This one goes and that one goes." Had her Galician poems been written in Castilian, Gerald Brenan declared, Rosalía de Castro would be recognized as "the greatest woman poet of modern times." Certainly they restored Galician, most musical of languages, to its ancient glory when it was the language of poetry on the Iberian peninsula, preferred even to Castilian. It is a question whether they could have been written in Castilian, for as John Frederick Nims comments, "sound and rhythm constitute their physical being"; and no other language, as Rosalía de Castro declared, has the sweetness and harmony of Galician. Moreover, they express quintessentially Galician emotions for which other languages lack words, for example, the sweet sadness of plaintive *saudade*, connoting solitude, longing for the absent, and a paradoxical comfort in the very melancholy it conveys.

The other poems included here are from her last book, *En las orillas del Saar* (*On the Shores of the River Saar*), written in Spanish and published in 1884, a few months before her death. According to Salvador de Madariaga, that volume establishes her poetry as "the best written in Spain in the nineteenth century."

Sor Juana Inés de la Cruz (Juana de Asbaje) (Mexico, 1648?–1695)

Juana de Asbaje was born in San Miguel Nepantla, a village at the foot of the volcano Popocatepétl, near Mexico City, when Mexico was part of the Spanish empire. Her mother was a native of Spanish descent, her father a Spaniard; as Spaniards did not marry natives, Juana de Asbaje was illegitimate. Having access to her maternal grandfather's library, she began reading and writing at three and composing verse at eight. As girls were barred from the University, she was largely self-educated, and with passionate intellectual drive amassed vast erudition in many fields. At sixteen, when news of her learning reached the Viceroy's palace, she was made lady-in-waiting to the Vicereine, and exhibited as a girl wonder.

In 1667, she sought escape in the austere order of Barefoot Carmelites, but finding its discipline too harsh, she joined the convent of St. Jerome in 1669, taking the name Sor Juana Inés de la Cruz. Though her prioress thought learning a matter for the Inquisition to investigate, Sor Juana filled her cell with some 4,000 books (one of the finest libraries in Mexico at the time). Here, she received her friends, painted, performed scientific experiments, and wrote philosophical, mathematical, musicological, and scientific treatises, often expressing dangerously unorthodox ideas. She wrote, directed, and sometimes acted in plays.

She also wrote poetry voluminously, in almost all the literary forms of the period: quatrains, *décimas*, romances, satires, *silvas*, sonnets, debates, carols, songs and *villancicos*. Her long philosophical poem ''Primero Sueño'' (''First Dream''), influenced by Góngora, establishes her as one of the principal poets in the Spanish language. We include here two of her baroque sonnets and a satiric poem against the unfairness of men's attitude toward women. Such arguments had been a popular form since the Middle Ages; known as the *tenso*, they were generally debates about love.

Sor Juana's *villancicos* are little known; ''Carol to Catherine,'' here translated for the first time, is among several dedicated to Catherine of Alexandria, for whom the Catherine Wheel was named. Catherine was one of the earliest (third century) Christian martyrs, and, in the long history of feminism, one of its first heroes. Like Sor Juana she was precocious and brilliant, devoting herself at an early age to science and philosophy, and to persuading the Emperor Maximinus to cease persecuting the Christians. To counter her arguments he confronted her with a panel of learned men, whom she instead converted. He finally decided to have her executed under a wheel with spikes protruding from the rim. Legend has it that the spikes flew off and killed the spectators instead, whereupon she was beheaded. Sor Juana's *villancicos* to St. Catherine, sung in the cathedral of Oaxaca in 1691, celebrated her triumph as a female intellect.

In her time Sor Juana gained wide recognition, but it was mainly in attempts to silence her and make her conform. Her response to the Bishop of Puebla, who asked her in 1693 to put aside her secular studies and devote more time to religious pursuits, constitutes a powerful declaration of the rights of women. In 1695 an epidemic broke out in Mexico City that killed 90 percent of the sisters in the convent. Sor Juana contracted the disease while nursing the victims and died April 17, 1695.

Rosario Ferré (Puerto Rico, 1940–)

"I was born in Ponce [Puerto Rico] and studied at Wellesley and Manhattanville colleges. I obtained my master's degree from the University of Puerto Rico. From 1970 to 1972 I edited the literary journal *Zona de Carga y Descarga*. I have published short stories and poetry: *Papeles de Pandora* (1976), *El medio pollito* (1978), *La muñeca menor* (1979), *Los cuentos de Juan Bobo* (1981), *Fabulas de la garza desangrada* (1982). In 1980 I published a collection of twelve essays devoted to women writers, *Sitio de Eros*, and a translation of Lillian Hellman's *Scoundrel Times*. I am the mother of three children and mistress of the home, and I do *not* write in order to make a living, but just out of necessity."

This brief autobiography leaves out a great deal: that Rosario Ferré long contributed a literary column to the newspaper *El Mundo*, that she has stimulated many young writers, and that she herself is one of Spanish America's most gifted narrators and poets.

Angela Figuera-Aymerich (Spain, 1902–1984)

Born in the Basque provinces, Angela Figuera-Aymerich spent her first twenty-seven years in the busy metropolis of Bilbao, where she attended a school having "100 boys and only 5 girls." After earning a degree in philosophy and literature, she taught in Huelva and Alcoy. Her marriage in 1934 produced a son.

In 1948 she published her first book of poems, *Mujer de barro*, inspired by love and maternity, followed by *Soria pura* (1949), evocations of the Soria region, which won the Premio Verbo. With *Vencida por el angel* (1950) she turned to the suffering world of the downtrodden, emphasized in *Los días duros*, *Víspera de la vida*, and *El grito inútil*, all collected in *Obras completas* (1952).

During the Spanish Civil War she wrote impassioned poems against Franco and Fascism, collected in *Belleza cruel*, first published in Mexico City in 1958 with an introduction by the Spanish poet-in-exile León-Felipe, who placed her among the outstanding poets of Spain. A memorable book for all time, it was reprinted in Barcelona in 1978 and became a best-seller. Her two-volume *Antología total*, published by the Editorial Afrodisio Aguado in 1975 and enlarged in 1978, has circulated widely throughout the Hispanic world.

Gloria Fuertes (Spain, 1918–)

As Gloria Fuertes describes her life, "I began to write before I learned to read. I recited my first poems to the kids in my neighborhood. Then I was taken to Radio España to recite my poems and later they took us all to war, which turned me into a pacifist and I went on writing for children."

Fuertes edited and contributed poems and stories to children's magazines from 1930 to 1950; she also wrote and produced two comedies for the children's theatre. During the Civil War, when she almost starved to death, she worked in a factory "showered every day with mortar shells." She got a job in the public library, where she "advised readers and smiled at them. My boss was The Book (*El libro*). I was free (*libre*)!"

In 1950 she published *Canciones para niños*, a volume of songs for children, as well as her first collection of poems, *Isla ignorada* (*Unknown Island*), which sold out rapidly. "We are impressed," said one critic, "not by what she has written here, but by what she is going to write." In 1954 she published *Aconsejo beber hilo* (*I Advise You to Drink Thread*) in Spain, and *Antología y poemas del suburbio* (*Anthology and Poems of the Slums*) in Venezuela. *Todo asusta*, which won first mention in the Concurso Internacional de Poesía Lírica Hispánica (in Venezuela), appeared in 1958. Three years later a Fulbright scholarship brought her to the United States, where at Bucknell University she taught "whatever I could and 20th century Spanish poetry."

Que estás en la tierra (*Who Art on Earth*) was published in 1962; *Ni tiro, ni veneno, ni navaja* (*Neither Gun nor Poison nor Razor*), which won the Premio Guipuzcoa, in 1965; *Poeta en guardia* (*Poet on Guard*) in 1968; *Cómo atar los bigotes al tigre* (*How to Tie the Tiger's Whiskers*) awarded an Accessit Premio Vizcaya, in 1969; and *Sola en la sala* (*Alone in the Living Room*) in 1973. Francisco Ynduráin collected her scattered works in *Antología poética 1950–1969*, reprinted every two years. Her *Obras incompletas*, edited by Fuertes herself, is now in its seventh edition (1981).

In her younger days, Fuertes broke tradition by wearing pants and riding a bicycle to work. Her colloquial poems—witty, spontaneous, charmingly sardonic—violate all the rules of the Academy, but her wordplay in the manner of Quevedo and Góngora is quintessentially Spanish and makes her hard to translate. The poem "I Make Poems, Gentlemen!", for example, is a tissue of untranslatable puns on the words *cosa* (thing), *caso* (case), and *casa* (house). Though not strictly a feminist, she writes from the woman's point of view, continually satirizing men, especially for their wars and other varieties of machismo. In addition to activities in the education of children, she has organized a society for training women to appreciate and express themselves in verse, called Versos con Faldas (Verses with Skirts).

Kyra Galván (Mexico, 1956–)

In her native Mexico City Kyra Galván wrote poetry "while she was still playing with her dolls," as Mercedes Durand notes in her introduction to Galván's *Un pequeño moretón en la piel de nadie* (1982), which won first prize in the Poesía Joven Francisco González de León. A "totally instinctive" fondness for choral music presaged her poetic vocation, which became fixed by age sixteen. At the university, however, she majored in political science because she "wanted to learn more about the social and economic relations which rule our lives: to learn more about money, social classes, . . . and history." Galván has published translations of Anna Akhmatova and Dylan Thomas and is now completing her second collection of poems.

Margarita Hickey (Spain, 1753–c.1791)
Daughter of an Irish army officer and an Italian singer, Margarita Hickey was born in Barcelona and brought at an early age to Madrid, where she lived most of her life. When very young she was married to a septuagenarian nobleman, who died in 1779. The beautiful young widow attracted numerous suitors, but her frustrations and bitter experiences became the subjects of her poetry, at first published under the pseudonym Antonia Hernanda de la Oliva and later her initials M.H.

She never married again, devoting her time to study, research and writing, especially in the field of geography. Her *Descripción geográfica e histórica de todo el orbe conocido hasta ahora* was rejected by the male-oriented Real Academia de la Historia and never published. Today she is best known for her translations of Racine's *Andromache* and Voltaire's *Zaïre,* as well as for her *Poesías varias sagradas, morales y profanas o amorosas* (1789).

Juana de Ibarbourou (Uruguay, 1895–1979)
Juana de Ibarbourou was born in the provincial town of Melo, Uruguay, on the Tacuarí River, of a Galician father, Vicente Fernández, and Uruguayan mother, Valentina Morales. Her formal training was limited to the local school, administered by nuns. She learned countless regional songs, and was enthralled when her father recited Rosalía de Castro's poems. At age fourteen she published her sonnet "El cordero" ("The Lamb") in the prestigious magazine *Atlántida.* Her marriage in 1915 to Captain Lucas Ibarbourou produced one son, Julio César.

Unlike most verse of the time, the poems in her collections, *Las lenguas de diamante* (1919), *El cántaro fresco* (1920), and *Raíz salvaje* (1922), were unaffected, spontaneous, and intensely erotic. After the death of her father in 1930 and her husband in 1942, she devoted herself to religious themes. Her works circulated so widely in Latin America she became known as "Juana de América." Juana de Ibarbourou was nominated several times for the Nobel Prize.

Raquel Jodorowsky (Chile, 1937–)
"I was born in a copper mine in Iquique, famous for its boxers. My father was a balalaika player who emigrated from Russia to the Chilean mines, my mother an illiterate woman who cut down a tree and made herself a plough and planted corn. I began to 'write' before I learned to read; and because dolls resembled dead children I preferred to play with spiders and lizards. I have written 14 books of poetry. I have a son and a parrot and

the whole world." Jodorowsky has lived much of her life in Peru, and is often considered a Peruvian writer, but she proudly calls herself "a daughter of David." Her volume *Caramelo de sal* (*Salt Candy*) appeared in 1981.

Elena Jordana (Argentina, 1940–)
Born in Buenos Aires, Elena Jordana lived in New York City from 1961 to 1972, and then in Buenos Aires and Mexico City. For a time, she ran a small press that published poets who, like herself, refused to kowtow to commercial publishers, as well as some of her favorite authors. In Mexico she won the Premio Nacional de Poesía de Aguascalientes for *Poemas no mandados* (1978), and the Premio Nacional de Letras Ramón López Velarde for her monologue *Mujer al sol* (1980). She says she writes to find relief, as a catharsis, and that she has been influenced by all the Hispanic poets, whether to come close to them or to escape them. She has two collections of unpublished poems, *La maga de Oz* and *9 Poemas a Don Juan*.

Susana March (Spain, 1918–)
Born in Barcelona, Susana March began publishing poems in magazines and newspapers before she was fifteen, and in 1938 gathered her verse in a collection entitled *Rutas*. Two years later she married novelist Ricardo Fernández de la Reguera. Her volumes *Ardiente voz* (1948) and *El viento de tristeza* (winner of the Premio Adonais in 1951), made her known throughout Spain. One of her novels, *Nina*, received the Premio Ciudad de Barcelona.

Josefa Masanés (Spain, 1811–1887)
Josefa Masanés, daughter of the prestigious cultural leader George Masanés of Tarragona, Spain, wrote in both Catalan and Spanish. Under her Catalan name, Maria Josepa Massanés i Dalmau, she was part of the Catalan literary renaissance, as it was referred to in 1857, especially after she won first prize in the Jocs Floral (Poetry Contest) of 1863 with "Creure ès viure." By then she was also known as a Spanish poet even in the United States, where her poem "El beso maternal" ("Mother's Kiss") of 1837 was recommended by the New York City Board of Education for use in public schools.

Masanés was much concerned with religion—as in her poem "Ana, madre de Samuel" (1848) and her play *Descenso de la Santísima Virgen a Barcelona* (1862)—and also with the education of the masses, as in her didactic poem *Importancia moral del Magisterio* (1858). Published volumes of poetry include *Poesías* (1841) and *Flores marchitas* (1850) in Spanish, and *Respirall* (1879) in Catalan.

In Masanés' day several gifted women writers were derided by male journalists as *femmes savantes* and *précieuses ridicules*. In "Resolution," here translated for the first time, Masanés defends them with a fine satiric humor.

Concha Michel (Mexico, 1899–)

In addition to songs, poems, plays, and an autobiography in *corrido* verse-form, Concha Michel has written extensively on the condition of Mexican women, and has worked for their improvement and education. In 1938 she published *Corridos revolucionarios* and the sociological study *Dos antagonismos fundamentales*. Her compilation *Cantos indígenas de México* (1951), with a prologue by Alfonso Pruneda, is Volume I of the prestigious Biblioteca del Folklore Indígena. She has also written essays on folkloric music.

Michel is one of the few poets to find inspiration in the ancient culture of the Mayas. In her poems *Génesis* and *Dios, Nuestra Señora*, published with other poems in 1966, she invokes the Mayan deity Ome-Teotl, the Dual-God, who unites harmoniously the feminine and masculine principles as expressed in the *Popol-Vuh*, the Bible of the Mayas. The political concept of a male God (Dios-Macho) arose, she claims, from the patriarchal capitalist system, which takes advantage of this ideology to reduce women to a secondary place and also exploits men. At present, Michel is finishing a new book.

Gabriela Mistral (Chile, 1889–1957)

Daughter of a poor schoolteacher, Lucila Godoy Alcayaga herself became a teacher (and later director) at elementary and secondary schools in various parts of Chile. At age eighteen she fell in love with a young railway worker, whose suicide two years later turned her to the writing of poetry. Under the pen name Gabriela Mistral she won first prize at the Juegos Florales of Santiago in 1914, for her "Sonetos de la muerte." Later poems, collected in *Desolación*, were published in New York in 1922, the year she was invited to reorganize the rural school system of Mexico. She published three more books of poetry: *Ternura* (1924), *Tala* (1938), and *Lagar* (1954). Some previously unpublished poems and prose works were collected by Gaston von dem Bussche and published by the Universidad Católica de Valparaiso in 1983. From 1925, she represented her country at the League of Nations, the United Nations, and also in Chilean consulates in Madrid, Lisbon, Rio de Janeiro, Nice, and Los Angeles.

Mistral is the only Latin American woman to have won the Nobel Prize (in 1945). She died in Hempstead, New York.

Nancy Morejón (Cuba, 1944–)

After working as a translator, Nancy Morejón became an editor for the Union of Cuban Writers and Artists, a position she holds today. She has published translations of Césaire, Roumain, and Depestre, among other poets, worked with various periodicals, and traveled and lectured widely throughout Europe, the United States, and Latin America. Her poems about women often reflect a profound indignation at past exploitation, particularly that of black women, and a confidence in a brighter future for them in her native Cuba.

Morejón's publications include *Mutismos* (1962), *Amor, ciudad atribuida* (1964), *Richard trajo su flauta* (which won an award in 1967), *Lengua de pájaro* (in collaboration with Carmen Gonce, 1967), *Parajes de una época* (1979), *Poemas* (1980), and *Octubre imprescindible* (1982). In addition to her *Recopilación de textos sobre Nicolás Guillén* (1974), she wrote an analysis of this poet, *Nación y mestizaje en Nicolás Guillén* (1982), that received the "Enrique José Varona" and "Mirta Aguirre" prizes for literary criticism.

A Nun from Alcalá (Spain, late seventeenth century)
Even during the apogee of mystical writing in Spain, veiled protests emanated from the nunneries. One of the most outspoken was a nun of the convent in Alcalá who lived in the late seventeenth century and left some "Décimas de una monja de Alcalá" ("Stanzas of a Nun of Alcalá"), from which this excerpt is taken. Her manuscript, two pages in quarto, is in the Biblioteca Nacional of Madrid.

Bertalicia Peralta (Panama, 1939–)
After studying music at the National Institute of Music and Journalism at the National University, Bertalicia Peralta taught for several years in secondary schools. She founded and co-edited *El Pez Original*, a magazine devoted to "new Panamanian writing," and contributed a column to the daily newspaper *Crítica*. She also organized a yearly children's literature contest.

Peralta's writings have won prizes in national and international contests and have been translated into several languages. Her poetry collections include: *Canto de esperanza filial* (1962), *Sendas fugitivas* (Ricardo Miró Prize, 1963), *Atrincherado amor* (1965), *Un lugar en la esfera terrestre* (third prize in the José Martí International Poetry Contest, 1971), *Ragul* (1976), *Casa flotante* (1979), and *Piel de gallina* (1982). She has also won prizes for her short stories, one of which, "Historia de la nube blanca y la semilla de mango," was adapted for Televisión Educativa. The plot for the ballet *El escondite del prófugo*, now in the repertoire of the Ballet Nacional de Panamá, was another of her creations.

In recognition of her cultural activities, the City of Panama declared her "Meritorious Daughter" and awarded her its keys.

Cristina Peri Rossi (Uruguay, 1941–)
After literary studies at the Instituto de Profesores Artigas, of Montevideo, Peri Rossi taught in various institutions and wrote for newspapers and magazines. She has published several volumes of short stories: *Viviendo* (1963), *Los museos abandonados* (1968), *Indicios pánicos* (1970), *La tarde del dinosaurio* (1976) and *La rebelión de los niños* (1976), which won her the Benito Pérez Galdós Prize, and a novel, *El libro de mis primos* (1969). As

a poet she won immediate recognition with *Ellos los bien nacidos* (1968), *Homenaje* (1968), and *Evohé* (1971). Peri Rossi has lived in exile in Barcelona since 1972; her four volumes published since have marked her as a leading voice in Spanish American poetry: *Descripción de un naufragio* (1974), an allegorical tale in verse depicting a shipwreck and reflecting her social milieu as well as her intimate life; *Diáspora* (1976), in which she draws an analogy between physical love and artistic creation; *Lingüística general* (1979), which won first prize in the Ciudad de Palma Poetry Contest; and *El deseo del bosque* (1980).

Florencia Pinar (Spain, c. 1460)
Florencia Pinar has been called the first woman who wrote poetry in Spanish under her own name. Actually, in Hernando del Castillo's *Cancionero* of 1511, which contains three of Pinar's "songs," the names of two other women are found, each with a *mote* or brief poetic motto or epigram. Little is known about her life except that she had a brother who glossed her songs and others in this collection, and wrote elaborate poems based on card games for the amusement of the aristocracy, attributed to "Pinar." They must have been close to if not a part of the court, possibly that of Isabel and Ferdinand, whose reign began in 1479. She was undoubtedly well educated.

We include here the second and third of the three poems by Florencia Pinar in the *Cancionero*. These have been much discussed in recent years, though formerly she was dismissed as an "erotic troubadour" of no great merit.

Benny Reyna (Panama, 1942–)
Verve and satiric malice run through the works of Bessy Reyna, one of her country's most promising younger poets. In *Terrarium* (1975) she collected a number of her poems that had been published in literary supplements and avant-garde magazines.

Alfonsina Storni (Argentina, 1892–1938)
From her birthplace in southern Switzerland, Alfonsina Storni was brought to Rosario, Argentina, at age three. An *enfant terrible*, she had a tempestuous childhood. As she describes it, "I grew up like a little animal, without supervision, swimming in the canals of San Juan, climbing quince trees, sleeping with my head pillowed in grapes." Her father died when she was fourteen, having taken to drink with the failure of his business enterprises. The following year she received a teacher's license in rural education, taught in Rosario, then joined a traveling theatre group. At nineteen she fell in love with a married man and bore him a son. To avoid embarrassing the father, she moved to Buenos Aires, where she tried to support herself and her child by working as teacher, actor, tutor, and clerk in an olive-oil importing firm, sometimes holding several jobs at once, and

all the while writing—poetry, articles, plays, novels—lecturing, and giving poetry recitals.

In 1916 her first book of poems appeared, *La inquietud del rosal,* followed in 1918 by *El dulce daño.* These early writings, romantic or modernist, failed to show her poetic potential, but with *Irremediablemente* (1919), *Languidez* (1920), and particularly *Ocre* (1925), in which she expressed her grievances with tremendous lyrical power, her full stature emerged. *Languidez* won the Primer Premio Municipal and the Segundo Premio Nacional; and Storni became a regular contributor to *La Nación.* In 1921, the city of Buenos Aires created the Teatro Infantil for her, so that she might write and direct children's plays. She also taught drama and speech at the Escuela Normal de Lenguas Vivas.

In 1926 she published *Poemas de amor,* and nine years later, her sixth book of verse, *Mundo de siete pozos* (1934). During those years, she taught at the Conservatorio de Música y Declamación, and saw her first play produced, *El amor del mundo.*

In 1935 she underwent a radical mastectomy from which she never recovered. Three years later her last book of poems appeared, *Mascarilla y trebol.* Finally, with constant pain in her arm, she could no longer write. Her last note, to her son, was dictated to a maid. Suspecting the cancer had spread to her lungs, she decided upon suicide. On a stormy night she dragged herself to the end of a pier in Mar del Plata and jumped into the waves.

Dolores Veintimilla de Galindo (Ecuador, 1830–1857)
Born in Quito, Ecuador, Dolores Veintimilla de Galindo showed her gifts at an early age in the town's intellectual circles. At fourteen she married a Colombian physician, Sixto Galindo, and set up house in Cuenca, Ecuador. Her early death came at the end of a tragic series of events, set in motion by her defense of a young Indian accused of murder. Bitterly attacked by her conservative provincial society, which regarded Indians as less than human, she became depressed and quite desolate. On the night of May 23, 1857, she burned all but a few of her poems and then poisoned herself.

Cecilia Vicuña (Chile, 1948–)
"My formal education began at the School of Architecture of the University of Chile but eventually I changed to the Escuela Nacional de Bellas Artes, obtaining my degree in Fine Arts in 1971. That year a British Council Scholarship took me to the Slade School of Fine Arts of the University College, London. In 1975 I obtained another scholarship from the Arts Council of Great Britain."

Vicuña's poems have appeared in many South American, European, and U.S. literary magazines. Some are collected in *Sabor a mi* (1973), published in London in a bilingual edition; *Siete poemas* (1979); in the bilingual

Precario/Precarious (1983), and in *Palabrarmas*, published in Buenos Aires in 1984. She is working on a bilingual series of Latin American poets to be called *Palabrasur*.

Idea Vilariño (Uruguay, 1920–)
Her father, a poet, loved poems and ideas, and named one of his daughters Poema and the other Idea. Signed Idea, Vilariño's first book, *La suplicante* (1945), contained only five short poems, all without punctuation; *Cielo, cielo* (1947) five more. *Paraíso perdido* (1949) contained these and a few others. In sympathy with the struggle against the Uruguayan regime, in 1951 she published *Por aire sucio* (*Through Dirty Air*); followed by *Nocturnos* (1955) and *Poemas de amor* (1958). Like many Latin American poets, Vilariño became politically active, and in the early sixties wrote stirring revolutionary folk songs, made popular by the singer René Zavaleta. She never considered them part of her oeuvre, however, and none are included in her published books of poetry. But they reached people her poems would never reach, she said, and to hear them sung gave her more pleasure than any of her published work, all written in an exceedingly condensed, elliptical style and dealing with love and death in a nihilistic manner reminiscent of Samuel Beckett. Shorn of all excess and pretense, her sparse poems gain maximum effect with seemingly minimal effort; their silences resound.

In 1973 a military coup in Uruguay defeated the opposition and eclipsed all cultural life. Denied outlets of expression, the intellectuals fled into exile, but Vilariño remained, in grim, solitary silence. In 1980 she published her latest collection of poems, *NO*, as well as *Segunda Antología*. Hers is "a poetry dealing with love and the feminine condition," writes the Argentine critic Luis Gregorovich, revealing "the tragic devaluation of woman and at the same time her profound superiority to man."

Adela Zamudio (Bolivia, 1854–1928)
Born in Cochabamba, Bolivia, Adela Zamudio attended public elementary school, following which she received tutoring from her father, Don Adolfo Zamudio, and mother, Doña Modesta Ribero de Zamudio. She taught at the Escuela San Alberto and later directed a girls' high school, now known as Liceo Adela Zamudio.

All her writings, poetry as well as fiction, deal with the social struggles of her country. Avoiding any form of religious fanaticism, she gave her revolt a boldly intellectual stance. In 1926 her native city awarded her the Crown of Distinction; today she is considered a precursor of South American feminism.

ACKNOWLEDGMENTS

We gratefully acknowledge permission to include the Spanish texts and English translations of the following poems:

CLARIBEL ALEGRÍA: "En la playa" and "Creí pasar mi tiempo." By permission of the poet.

ANONYMOUS: "Delgadina" translated by Lysander Kemp and "Now That I'm Young" and "That I'm Ill Married" translated by William M. Davis from *An Anthology of Medieval Lyrics*, ed. by Angel Flores. New York: Modern Library, 1962. © 1962 by Angel Flores.

SOR JUANA INÉS DE LA CRUZ: "On Her Portrait" translated by Kate Flores and "Arguing That There Are Inconsistencies between Men's Tastes and Their Censure When They Accuse Women of What They Themselves Do Cause" translated by Muriel Kittel from *An Anthology of Spanish Poetry from Garcilaso to García Lorca*, ed. by Angel Flores. Garden City, N.Y.: Anchor Books, Doubleday, 1961. © 1961 by Angel Flores.

CECILIA BELLI: Excerpts from "Canto al Nuevo Tiempo." By permission of the poet.

JULIA DE BURGOS: "A Julia de Burgos" from her *Obra poética*. Río Piedras, Puerto Rico: Ediciones Huracán, 1961. By permission of the publisher.

ROSARIO CASTELLANOS: "Se habla de Gabriel," "Jornada de la soltera," and "Meditación en el umbral" from her volume *Poesía eres tu*. Mexico City: Editorial Joaquin Mortiz, 1972. By permission of Fondo de Cultura Económica, Mexico City.

JUANA CASTRO: "María Encadenada" from her volume *Cóncava mujer*. Córdoba, Spain: Grupo Zubia, 1978. © by Juana Castro. By permission of the poet.

ROSALIA DE CASTRO: "From the Cadenced Roar of the Waves" and "Feeling Her End Would Come with Summer's End" translated by Kate Flores from *An Anthology of Spanish Poetry from Garcilaso to García Lorca*, ed. by Angel Flores. Garden City, N.Y.: Anchor Books, Doubleday, 1961. © 1961 by Angel Flores.

ROSARIO FERRÉ: "Envío" from her volume *Fabulas de la garza desangrada*. Mexico City: Editorial Joaquin Mortiz, 1982. © 1982 by Rosario Ferré. By permission of the poet.

ANGELA FIGUERA-AYMERICH: "Madres," "Destino," and "Mujeres del mercado" from *Poesía femenina española, 1930–1950*, 2nd ed., ed. by Carmen Conde. Barcelona: Editorial Bruguera, 1970. By permission of the publisher.

GLORIA FUERTES: "No sé," "No dejan escribir," "Hagan versos, señores!" "Tener un hijo hoy" and "Los pájaros anidan en mis brazos" from her *Obras incompletas*, 7th ed. Madrid: Ediciones Cátedra, 1981. © by Gloria Fuertes. By permission of the poet.

KYRA GALVÁN: "Contradicciones ideológicas al lavar un plato" from her volume *Un pequeño moretón en la piel de nadie*. Mexico City: Ediciones Contraste, 1982. © 1982 by Kyra Galván. By permission of the poet.

JUANA DE IBARBOUROU: "Rebelde" and "¡Mujer!" from her volume *Los mejores poemas*. Montevideo: Arca Editorial, 1968. By permission of the publisher.

RAQUEL JODOROWSKY: "No me relaciono," "Aquí estamos," and "El secreto" from her volume *Caramelo de sal*. Privately printed, Lima, Peru, 1981. By permission of the poet.

ELENA JORDANA: "Tango" from her volume *Poemas no mandados*. Mexico City: Editorial Joaquin Mortiz, 1979. By permission of the poet.

SUSANA MARCH: "A un hombre" from *Poesía femenina española, 1930–1950*, 2nd ed., ed. by Carmen Conde. Barcelona: Editorial Bruguera, 1970. By permission of the publisher.

The Feminist Press at the City University of New York offers alternatives in education and in literature. Founded in 1970, this non-profit, tax-exempt educational and publishing organization works to eliminate sexual stereotypes in books and schools and to provide literature with a broad vision of human potential. The publishing program includes reprints of important works by women, feminist biographies of women, and nonsexist children's books. Curricular materials, bibliographies, directories, and a quarterly journal provide information and support for students and teachers of women's studies. In-service projects help to transform teaching methods and curricula. Through publications and projects, The Feminist Press contributes to the rediscovery of the history of women and the emergence of a more humane society.

FEMINIST CLASSICS FROM THE FEMINIST PRESS

Antoinette Brown Blackwell: A Biography, by Elizabeth Cazden. $19.95 cloth, $9.95 paper.
Between Mothers and Daughters: Stories Across a Generation. Edited by Susan Koppelman. $8.95 paper.
Brown Girl, Brownstones, a novel by Paule Marshall. Afterword by Mary Helen Washington. $8.95 paper.
Call Home the Heart, a novel of the thirties, by Fielding Burke. Introduction by Alice Kessler-Harris and Paul Lauter and afterwords by Sylvia J. Cook and Anna W. Shannon. $8.95 paper.
Cassandra, by Florence Nightingale. Introduction by Myra Stark. Epilogue by Cynthia Macdonald. $3.50 paper.
The Changelings, a novel by Jo Sinclair. Afterwords by Nellie McKay; and by Johnnetta B. Cole and Elizabeth H. Oakes; biographical note by Elisabeth Sandberg. $8.95 paper.
The Convert, a novel by Elizabeth Robins. Introduction by Jane Marcus. $6.95 paper.
Daughter of Earth, a novel by Agnes Smedley. Afterword by Paul Lauter. $7.95 paper.
A Day at a Time: The Diary Literature of American Women from 1764 to the Present, edited and with an introduction by Margo Culley. $29.95 cloth, $12.95 paper.
The Defiant Muse: French Feminist Poems from the Middle Ages to the Present, a bilingual anthology edited and with an introduction by Domna C. Stanton. $29.95 cloth, $11.95 paper.
The Defiant Muse: German Feminist Poems from the Middle Ages to the Present, a bilingual anthology edited and with an introduction by Susan L. Cocalis. $29.95 cloth, $11.95 paper.
The Defiant Muse: Hispanic Feminist Poems from the Middle Ages to the Present, a bilingual anthology edited and with an introduction by Angel Flores and Kate Flores. $29.95 cloth, $11.95 paper.
The Defiant Muse: Italian Feminist Poems from the Middle Ages to the Present, a bilingual anthology edited by Beverly Allen, Muriel Kittel, and Keala Jane Jewell, and with an introduction by Beverly Allen. $29.95 cloth, $11.95 paper.
The Female Spectator, edited by Mary R. Mahl and Helene Koon. $8.95 paper.
Guardian Angel and Other Stories, by Margery Latimer. Afterwords by Nancy Loughridge, Meridel Le Sueur, and Louis Kampf. $8.95 paper.
I Love Myself When I Am Laughing...And Then Again When I Am Looking Mean and Impressive, by Zora Neale Hurston. Edited by Alice Walker with an introduction by Mary Helen Washington. $9.95 paper.
Käthe Kollwitz: Woman and Artist, by Martha Kearns. $7.95 paper.
Life in the Iron Mills and Other Stories, by Rebecca Harding Davis. Biographical interpretation by Tillie Olsen. $7.95 paper.
The Living Is Easy, a novel by Dorothy West. Afterword by Adelaide M. Cromwell. $8.95 paper.
The Other Woman: Stories of Two Women and a Man. Edited by Susan Koppelman. $8.95 paper.
Mother to Daughter, Daughter to Mother: A Daybook and Reader, selected and shaped by Tillie Olsen. $9.95 paper.
Portraits of Chinese Women in Revolution, by Agnes Smedley. Edited with an introduction by Jan MacKinnon and Steve MacKinnon and an afterword by Florence Howe. $5.95 paper.
Reena and Other Stories, selected short stories by Paule Marshall. $8.95 paper.
Ripening: Selected Work, 1927–1980, by Meridel Le Sueur. Edited with an introduction by Elaine Hedges. $8.95 paper.

Rope of Gold, a novel of the thirties, by Josephine Herbst. Introduction by Alice Kessler-Harris and Paul Lauter and afterword by Elinor Langer. $8.95 paper.

The Silent Partner, a novel by Elizabeth Stuart Phelps. Afterword by Mari Jo Buhle and Florence Howe. $8.95.

Swastika Night, a novel by Katharine Burdekin. Introduction by Daphne Patai. $8.95 paper.

These Modern Women: Autobiographical Essays from the Twenties. Edited with an introduction by Elaine Showalter. $4.95 paper.

The Unpossessed, a novel of the thirties, by Tess Slesinger. Introduction by Alice Kessler-Harris and Paul Lauter and afterword by Janet Sharistanian. $8.95 paper.

Weeds, a novel by Edith Summers Kelley. Afterword by Charlotte Goodman. $7.95 paper.

A Woman of Genius, a novel by Mary Austin. Afterword by Nancy Porter. $8.95 paper.

The Woman and the Myth: Margaret Fuller's Life and Writings, by Bell Gale Chevigny. $8.95 paper.

Women and Appletrees, a novel by Moa Martinson. Translated from the Swedish and with an afterword by Margaret S. Lacy. $8.95 paper.

The Yellow Wallpaper, by Charlotte Perkins Gilman. Afterword by Elaine Hedges. $4.50 paper.

OTHER TITLES FROM THE FEMINIST PRESS

Black Foremothers: Three Lives, by Dorothy Sterling. $8.95 paper.

All The Women Are White, All The Blacks Are Men, But Some of Us Are Brave: Black Women's Studies. Edited by Gloria T. Hull, Patricia Bell Scott, and Barbara Smith. $12.95.

Complaints and Disorders: The Sexual Politics of Sickness, by Barbara Ehrenreich and Deirdre English. $3.95 paper.

The Cross-Cultural Study of Women. Edited by Margot I. Duley and Mary I. Edwards. $29.95 cloth, $12.95 paper.

Feminist Resources for Schools and Colleges: A Guide to Curricular Materials, 3rd edition. Compiled and edited by Anne Chapman. $12.95 paper.

Household and Kin: Families in Flux, by Amy Swerdlow et al. $8.95 paper.

How to Get Money for Research, by Mary Rubin and the Business and Professional Women's Foundation. Foreword by Mariam Chamberlain. $6.95 paper.

In Her Own Image: Women Working in the Arts. Edited with an introduction by Elaine Hedges and Ingrid Wendt. $9.95 paper.

Integrating Women's Studies into the Curriculum: A Guide and Bibliography, by Betty Schmitz. $9.95 paper.

Las Mujeres: Conversations from a Hispanic Community, by Nan Elsasser, Kyle MacKenzie, and Yvonne Tixier y Vigil. $8.95 paper.

Lesbian Studies: Present and Future. Edited by Margaret Cruikshank. $9.95 paper.

Moving the Mountain: Women Working for Social Change, by Ellen Cantarow with Susan Gushee O'Malley and Sharon Hartman Strom. $8.95 paper.

Out of the Bleachers: Writings on Women and Sport. Edited with an introduction by Stephanie L. Twin. $9.95 paper.

Reconstructing American Literature: Courses, Syllabi, Issues. Edited by Paul Lauter. $10.95 paper.

Salt of the Earth, screenplay by Michael Wilson with historical commentary by Deborah Silverton Rosenfelt. $5.95 paper.

Witches, Midwives, and Nurses: A History of Women Healers, by Barbara Ehrenreich and Deirdre English. $3.95 paper.

With These Hands: Women Working on the Land. Edited with an introduction by Joan M. Jensen. $9.95 paper.

Woman's "True" Profession: Voices from the History of Teaching. Edited with an introduction by Nancy Hoffman. $9.95 paper.

Women Have Always Worked: A Historical Overview, by Alice Kessler-Harris. $8.95 paper.

Women Working: An Anthology of Stories and Poems. Edited and with an introduction by Nancy Hoffman and Florence Howe. $8.95 paper.

For free catalog, write to The Feminist Press at the City University of New York, 311 East 94 Street, New York, N.Y. 10128. Send individual book orders to The Feminist Press, P.O. Box 1654, Hagerstown, MD 21741. Include $1.75 postage and handling for one book and 75¢ for each additional book. To order using MasterCard or Visa, call: (800) 638-3030.